NOT
FORGOTTEN

Not
FORGOTTEN

INSPIRING MISSIONARY PIONEERS

DAVID J. BRADY

XULON PRESS

Xulon Press
2301 Lucien Way #415
Maitland, FL 32751
407.339.4217
www.xulonpress.com

Xulon
PRESS

Unless otherwise indicated, Scripture quotations taken from the English Standard Version (ESV). Copyright © 2001 by Crossway, a publishing ministry of Good News Publishers. Used by permission. All rights reserved.

Printed in the United States of America.

ISBN-13: 978-1-54564-206-1

THIS BOOK IS DEDICATED TO
the first missionaries I ever knew and loved
Mom and Dad.

Martha Yates Brady and Otis W. Brady
faithfully served the Lord for forty years as
Southern Baptist missionaries.
Their beautiful commitment to
Christ and His Great Commission
inspires me every day.

CONTENTS

Introduction ix

1. John Lake: Founder of Tai-Kam Island Leper Colony 1
2. Samuel Clopton: The First Southern Baptist Missionary ... 19
3. Charles Gaillard: Tragedy Made Beautiful 33
4. Lough Fook: Morningstar of the Chinese Missions
   Movement......................................41
5. Otis Brady: Church Planter in Caribbean Lands.......... 49
6. John Day: Pioneer African-American Baptist
   Missionary to Liberia...............................65
7. Thomas Jefferson Bowen: The David Livingstone of
   Southern Baptists...................................75
8. Mary Reid: Though He Slay Me, Yet Will I Trust Him 91
9. Matthew Yates: Towering Pioneer of Southern Baptist
   Missions 97
10. Landrum Holmes: The First Southern Baptist
    Missionary Murdered............................... 109
11. Sallie Holmes: Faithful Through Deep and Dark Waters .. 119
12. Sarah Rohrer: First Southern Baptist Missionaries
    Appointed to Japan.................................127
13. Solomon Ginsburg: Unlikely Southern Baptist
    Missionary to Brazil............................... 133
14. Erik Nelson: Pioneer of Baptist Missions in the Amazon.. 143
15. George Lacy: Theological Educator and Faithful
    Sufferer in Mexico 159
16. T.W. Ayers: Pioneer Medical Missionary 169
17. William Enete: Missionary Ventriloquist 185
18. Lula Whilden: Evangelist to Destitute Women..........197

Acknowledgements..................................... **209**
Photograph Credits **211**

INTRODUCTION

I remember the moment that *Not Forgotten: Inspiring Missionary Pioneers* first came to life. I was standing at the Wall of Witnesses, which commemorates Southern Baptist missionaries who died during their years of service. I knew very few of the names. However, I had just read a quote by one of them, a missionary from the 1800s, whose ship disappeared en route to her field of service. Sarah Robinson Rohrer was the only child of her widowed mother. Sarah's mother was distraught that her twenty-four-year-old daughter was leaving for missionary service in Japan. She begged her not to go. Sarah responded, ***"Mother, with the exception of parting from you, this is the happiest day of my life, if we are lost at sea, death will find us in the path of duty."***

When I read these words, I was overwhelmed with emotion and exclaimed, "A woman like that cannot be forgotten! Her story must be told! We need to remember her and her commitment to Jesus Christ!" Little did I realize, God had just shown me the path of duty—writing this book. Over the past two years, I have had the privilege of getting to know (through books and letters) scores of Southern Baptist missionaries. I have been inspired by the depth of their faith, challenged by the breadth of their labors, and brought to tears by their sufferings. I want you to meet these missionaries. As you get to know them, I believe you will be strengthened as I have been.

Although the fruit of each missionary's life looks different, they all share—without exception—the same root: Jesus Christ! He is the real hero of these stories. These men and women were His ambassadors. They were saved by Him, sent out by Him, empowered by Him, made fruitful by Him, and ultimately, brought home *to* Him. Their lives matter much because they lived for Him, who matters most. In the words of the first Southern Baptist missionary, Samuel Clopton, *"Let Jesus command, and I delight to obey!"* The commission of Christ to go and make disciples of all nations became a personal imperative to each of these missionaries.

As Southern Baptists, we are a missionary people. Since 1845, the core of our identity has been missions. Together we have sent out almost 25,000 missionaries. Sadly, the average Southern Baptist can name very few of them beyond Lottie Moon. In this book, I introduce you to eighteen inspiring missionary pioneers. Some of them were well known during their lifetime, and others have never been well known. Each person selected spoke to my heart. Hopefully, they will speak to yours.

In the course of researching these men and women, I was interested to learn that many of them were inspired to missions by reading a missionary biography. I have endeavored to make these stories personally engaging and historically accurate. However, I am sure despite my best efforts, some errors have made their way into the book. The constant reference to dates may be bothersome to some readers, but history without dates becomes a muddle. In my opinion, the best part of the book is hearing our missionaries speak in their own words. The missionary quotes are in *italics* to help you easily identify them. Each chapter can stand alone as its own story; however, there are several that form a larger story (be on the lookout).

Interacting with the men and women in these pages has made me want to be a better personal evangelist and more supportive of our missionaries. Above all, I want *my* life to count for Christ's glory. Prayerfully, this book will inspire you to greater obedience to the Great Commission. Happy reading!

David J. Brady
Shadowlands Farm
June 2018

John and Carrie Lake

Chapter One

JOHN LAKE

1870-1949
Founder of Tai-Kam Island Leper Colony

"The blind receive their sight and the lame walk,
lepers are cleansed..."   **Matthew 11:5a**

J ohn Lake saw the beautiful green mountains rising out of the
sea. He was not only enthralled by those scattered island jewels,
but also by the fact that he was seeing them from an airplane. His
pilot was a Frenchman named Captain Ricou, who had been a
flying ace in World War I. This flight on June 18, 1920, is one
of the first recorded by a Southern Baptist missionary. Lake was
surveying the islands in the South China Sea between Macau and
Hong Kong in search of a home for the lepers to whom he had been
ministering for years.

There were an estimated one million lepers in South China at
that time, and they were the most despised and mistreated of all
people. John Lake, however, loved lepers and hoped that his love
would open a door for many of them to trust Christ as their Savior.
Contracting leprosy meant immediate social death and a slow, gru-
eling physical death. The ravages of that dread disease were evident

in the hands and feet that were missing and the noses, eyes, ears, and lips that were so horribly disfigured. These lepers had been cast out of their communities and forced to live in isolation and grinding poverty. Yet, the command of Christ to **"heal the sick and cleanse the lepers"** had taken hold of Lake's heart and hands. He was determined to find a way to help them.

Since 1910, Lake had been making visits to lepers in the delta region south of the Pearl River. He brought them food, clothes, Bibles, and tracts. The lepers begged him to help them find a home near water, so they could provide for themselves by fishing. A prominent Chinese friend suggested that an island off the coast might be a good solution. Lake began making trips to explore those islands. One island was Shangchuang where Jesuit missionary Francis Xavier died in 1552, while attempting to enter mainland China. China was completely closed to Christianity and outsiders. Xavier exclaimed, as he lay dying of fever off the forbidden coast, "O rock, rock! When wilt thou open?" Another rocky island was in plain view of Shangchuang. Unlike Shangchuang, it was largely uninhabited and seemed promising. Lake was disappointed when told it would not be possible to visit that island because it was a hideout for pirates.

A few months later, the officials changed their minds and escorted Lake to the island of Tai-Kam aboard a Chinese Navy gunboat. As Lake neared the rocky island of Tai-Kam, he remembered Francis Xavier's words and issued his response, *"O Rock, thy heart hath opened! Mine is full, And overflowing, with its song of praise!"* Lake was captivated and exuberantly reported, *"The island a little less than three miles from shore, has about eight square miles, some of it now under cultivation; and the hills that form its eastern, northern, and western border, are well wooded. One stream of fresh water, over a mile long, with several smaller streams will furnish enough water for a leper colony with several thousand people."*

The problem still standing in the way—pirates! In a bold move, Lake decided to speak with them directly. The pirates lived in a village two and a half miles away from where Lake desired to build a home for the lepers. Lake said, *"The inhabitants of the one fishing village on the island, some of whom are pirates of the worst type— but the pirates, like the rest, listened to the Gospel, and showed us many courtesies. God grant that ere long they may become our brothers in Christ and our allies in our work for the lepers."* Lake slowly began to win over the pirates, and he offered them construction jobs in the proposed colony.

On the mainland, Lake visited his good friend, Wu Ting-fang, and asked him to help with the acquisition of Tai-Kam. Dr. Wu, a lawyer and government official, who had been China's envoy to the USA, gave him $5,000 for the purchase of the entire island. Lake rejoiced, *"God has overruled the mighty obstacles, one by one, and this lovely island is ours!"* The local government gave the mission a boat, confiscated from smugglers, and the missionaries named it *The Alice.* As additional money came in, the pirates went to work erecting numerous stone and brick buildings, as well as a pier for boat arrivals. It took several years, but finally, small groups of lepers were transported to their new island home: Tai-Kam.

Although Lake's plans for a colony of thousands did not come to pass, over the next twenty-five years, hundreds of lepers did come to live on Tai-Kam. All of the funds for the projects came from private donors, and the colony was built "in spite of pirates, typhoons and stormy seas, adverse criticism and opposition, financial problems, civil strife, strikes and boycotts." The buildings were simple and solid with a church standing prominently in the center of the village. Each Lord's Day, it was filled with worshipers, "and pirates often attended services in the new chapel, sitting in the gallery listening intently, and in later years **a former pirate became a pastor to the lepers**."

Eventually, there were fifty buildings in the colony. There were vegetable gardens, and they raised poultry, sheep, goats, and hogs. There was a medical clinic and a dispensary to meet the many needs of the residents. The long-ago request for a home where the lepers could fish was met beyond their wildest dreams. Fish and more fish were always available, just a cast away. A visitor to the island exulted, "In nature's sunny moods the wealth of colour here furnishes a living canvas... A kingfisher may be seen skimming lightly by, dipping his feet into the deep blue waters, while the pulsating red of flowering plants on the hills above, and the yellows and purples of irises below, quiver, like the rippled sea beyond, in the faint morning breeze." Tai-Kam felt like an earthly paradise. The lepers knew they were incredibly blessed to call it home. Lake wrote numerous poems; one entitled "Tai-Kam" concludes:

And now I love to walk with Him and His,
Among these island-mountain mysteries;
And so, in lowly ministry, to find
Communion sweet, with God and humankind
While robbers find the Christ upon the cross,
And lepers, cleansed, forget their pain and loss.

Lake knew that the deepest need of every man and woman is to know God as his or her Father through the Son, Jesus Christ. The Gospel was preached, and the Da Kum Baptist Church was planted on Tai-Kam. Many years later, the members of the church wrote to Lake in America:

> By the great Grace of God and your kindness and love in building the hospital to take care of our deformed bodies; and moreover, in establishing the Church to open up our eyes and ears, both our bodies and souls are benefitted. This is, indeed, a great good fortune in the midst of misfortune. Your labors, both physical and mental, have been unceasing wherever you went in order to raise funds for the hospitals so that we lepers would be prevented from starving to death. Your kindness is, indeed, even greater than that of our own blood fathers. We therefore, hold a birthday celebration on February 11(humorously, his birthday was June 11) every year to honor you.... All members of the church, blessed by the true God and the Holy Ghost, have been very devoted to the Gospel.

At that point there were one hundred and five members of the church. All lepers, regardless of their religion or lack thereof, were welcome on the island, and none was pressured to attend church or to believe, but all heard the Gospel with their ears and saw the fruit of the Gospel with their eyes. And by God's grace, over the years many turned to the leper-cleansing Jesus in saving faith.

What do we know about John Lake, the founder and guiding spirit of Tai-Kam Leper Colony? Lake was born June 11, 1870, in Edgefield County, South Carolina. As the first of twelve children, he was born prematurely but miraculously lived. John had to take a leading role in his family from a very early age because his father had been wounded in the Civil War. At sixteen he was converted to Christ and ordained to the Gospel ministry by the First Baptist Church of Edgefield. He won a scholarship to the South Carolina Military College (The Citadel) in Charleston, where he completed his degree in three years. While in college, he was impacted by evangelist Dwight L. Moody and the Student Volunteer Movement.

In 1888, he dedicated his life to serve as a foreign missionary *wherever*, and *however*, God directed. Two years later while recuperating from illness, he borrowed a copy of the recently published *The Lepers of Molokai*. This poignant story presented the life and ministry of Father Damien, a Belgian Roman Catholic priest, as he ministered to lepers on the Hawaiian island of Molokai. Young Lake was deeply moved and believed he was called by God to carry out a similar ministry saying, *"If a Catholic priest could do this, so could a Baptist minister."*

Upon graduation he returned to his hometown where he helped organize the Edgefield Chapter of the YMCA and served as pastor in several rural churches in the county. The door opened for him to travel to China under the auspices of the YMCA. There he worked with international sailors that passed through the city of Canton (Guangzhou). He began the process of learning Chinese and was also appointed as a Southern Baptist missionary in 1903. At the suggestion of the venerable veteran missionary, Dr. Rosewell H. Graves, he commenced work in the Siyi (Four Provinces) region

6

in the Pearl River Delta of southern Guangdong. Lake served as a general evangelist for almost twenty years, traveling extensively through this region to plant and strengthen churches.

In 1907, at the age of thirty-seven, Lake married Pearl Hall; less than one year later, she became ill and died. In 1909, he married Carrie Bostick, a graduate of Greenville Female College (now merged with Furman University). She taught there for ten years prior to becoming a missionary to China in 1901. Carrie was always John's *"Little Lady of the Lake"* and constant companion. She ministered in countless ways and was a rock of support in establishing Tai-Kam Leper Colony.

In 1928, when John and Carrie had just returned to their home in Canton from Tai-Kam, they described their journey as *"incomparably our happiest trip, and those our happiest days, up to then."* Carrie complained of not feeling well, and there was a sudden and alarming rise in her temperature. A doctor and three nurses sought to help her. John also fell ill, and it was clear they both had malaria. Loving, praying friends kept vigil for them, but Carrie's body grew weaker. As she expired, John, with trembling lips, whispered into her ear, *"Good by, good by.... Meet me sometime on Tai-Kam Island."*

John recovered quickly from the malaria but not so quickly from the grief. He moved out to Tai-Kam to be comforted by his leper brothers and sisters; yet, his sorrow at the death of Carrie continued. He wrote:

> *Sad mystery of loneliness! No eye*
> *To drink with mine the glory of the sky*
> *When sank the sun behind that golden sea;*

No ear to hear God's evensong with me;
No trusting heart, transforming with its love,
And lifting mine to rhapsodies above
Alone, alone, beyond earth's furthest shore
And night is falling! Oh, what more, what more?

The leper colony needed financial assistance, so Lake returned to America to tell its story and seek donors. During this time he fell in love with a young woman from North Carolina, who was enrolled at the Women's Missionary Training School in Louisville, Kentucky. Her name was Virginia Lake, and she was his thirteenth cousin! They married in 1933—when John was sixty-three years old—and went to China together. They had two daughters, Virginia and Rosa, and the Lakes continued to work for the good of the lepers of Tai-Kam. John Lake was a gifted speaker and traveled around the world four times telling the story of Tai-Kam. On one visit to the USA, Lake was in a serious automobile accident and broke his back. Sadly, he was never able to return to China, but he lived the rest of his days advocating for the lepers of Tai-Kam. Physicians told Lake that he should rest and take care of himself. He interpreted that to mean, *"Go as far and as fast as I can, speak once, twice, or more times every day, and arouse the churches for the cause of foreign missions everywhere!"*

World War II cut off all communication with Tai-Kam. The Japanese occupied the entire region. Lake longed to hear from the lepers, but all was silent. World War II ended, but still no word was heard. Not long before Lake's death, missionary Rex Ray contacted him saying, "At night we rowed across the open sea to the leper colony and the hospital on Tai Kam Island. Just before sunrise we dropped anchor. I blew a big conk-shell horn. The lepers on shore responded by singing songs of praise to the Lord.... There were **only three survivors** out of more than a hundred lepers on the island when the Japanese attacked."

Almost a hundred lepers had been massacred on their beautiful island home. Lake had worked to provide them with safety, but evil had invaded paradise. Lake had prepared the lepers and pirates for such a day by faithfully teaching them about the True Home — the home into which no darkness, disease, disaster, or death can invade. Lake lived and preached, *"here we have no lasting city, but we seek the city that is to come."* If we only give people a better home on earth, but do not prepare them for their eternal home, we have failed.

This theme of *home* permeated Lake's mind as he lay dying at the age of seventy-nine. He saw death as journeying home to the Father's house where there are many mansions. Lake died on August 28, 1949, in Kansas City, Missouri, and his body was transported to Edgefield, South Carolina, where he was buried with a large rock from Tai-Kam marking the spot.

What happened to Tai-Kam after the communist takeover? All missionaries were forced out of China. Darkness again fell over Tai-Kam Island, and nothing was heard for decades. Only recently has what transpired come to light. The communists retained Tai-Kam as a place for lepers, changing its official name to Dajin Island, but its common name was simply, Leprosy Island. The old and most seriously ill lepers from the mainland were taken there. They received very little support, and the island became more like a forgotten prison than an island of hope.

In the 1980s, the terrible conditions of the lepers on the island came to the attention of Fr. Luis Ruiz, a Spanish priest, who was living and ministering in Macau. Fr. Ruiz traveled to the leper colony and was moved with compassion to help. He made massive efforts to bring much-needed clothes, food, and medicines to the island. As the conditions improved, Ruiz realized that the lepers still lacked something. What they lacked was love! He invited the Catholic Sisters from India to care for the patients. These nuns have made a wonderful difference in the lives of the lepers, bringing care and love to each one.

The buildings constructed by Lake are still being used, but apparently, his story has been forgotten. Tracing the hand of Providence is difficult; yet, God's smile can *almost* be discerned at Catholics now running a leper colony started by a Baptist who was inspired by a Catholic. Above all, we see that the mercy of the LORD endures forever. AMEN.

*The next four photographs are:

Tai-Kam Leper Colony under construction

Tai-Kam Island from boat

Tai-Kam residents

Tai-Kam men waving

John Lake

John Lake

Chapter Two

SAMUEL CLOPTON

1816-1847
The First Southern Baptist Missionary

"Go therefore and make disciples of all nations, bap-
tizing them in the name of the Father and of the Son
and of the Holy Spirit, teaching them to observe all
that I have commanded you. And behold, I am with
you always, to the end of the age."

Matthew 28:19-20

How did Samuel Cornelius Clopton become the first
Southern Baptist missionary appointed by the Foreign
Mission Board? He was appointed in September 1845, but many
substantial steps had been taken before he arrived at that day.

His father and grandfather were both Baptist pastors. His grandfather, William Clopton, is described as a "faithful preacher of the
gospel." He and his wife were intent on raising their children in the
fear and admonition of the Lord. His son, James Clopton (Samuel's
father), followed in his footsteps and became a pastor in New Kent
County, Virginia. He served several congregations, but his primary
field of labor was as pastor of Emmaus (pronounced "Emmy-us" by

locals) Baptist Church. He was a solid—not flashy—preacher and pastor, and James B. Taylor said of him, "By evenness of temper and habitual consistency of character, he adorned the doctrine of God his Saviour, compelling all to see and admit the power of that doctrine to sanctify and save."

Samuel C. Clopton was born January 7, 1816. He was James Clopton's third son. Church was a central part of his upbringing, and from his earliest days, he attended services where he heard his father proclaim God's great salvation for sinners through Jesus Christ. In their home, prayer was a daily part of family life, and it served to inculcate a deep spiritual interest in young Samuel's mind and heart. He was known for his fervent prayers to God and his seriousness about life. In 1833, at the age of seventeen, Samuel was converted to God, placing his trust in Jesus Christ. Interestingly, James B. Taylor, who became the first Corresponding Secretary of the Foreign Mission Board, baptized him. Most of what we know about Samuel comes from the pen of Taylor, who later said about Southern Baptists' first missionary, "Everything connected with the being of this man is wrapped in mystery. That he should exist at all is mysterious. All the events of his history are wonderful; and, when he passes away, all seems more like a dream than reality."

Six years later in 1839, Samuel began to ponder whether God might be calling him into the ministry. In his journal entry for Sunday, May 12, 1839, he says, *"Having read five chapters in the Testament, and a chapter in Josephus, I went to Sunday-school, and taught until eleven o'clock, at which time we engaged in a prayer-meeting. Being called upon to lead in prayer, I did so; and after awhile, being requested to give a word of exhortation, I tried to do it; but it being the first time I ever attempted to do such a thing, I felt a little agitated at first. If I did wrong, Lord, forgive all."*

As Clopton began to receive invitations to speak in various churches, it confirmed his sense of calling. By May of 1842, Samuel had fully embraced God's call to be an ambassador for Jesus Christ. In his journal he states, *"I have had a clearer view of the plan of salvation than ever before. How I love to think of the position my Saviour took on behalf of a lost world. If I could, I would submit a thousand souls, if I had them, in his hands. When I view the plan of salvation as it is, I want to be explaining it to my fellowmen."*

Samuel was now convinced that in order to increase his usefulness for Christ, he needed to prepare his mind as well as his spirit. He attended Richmond College for two years, Columbian College for two years, and Newton Theological School for two years. During his course of studies, he sought every opportunity to minister in local churches and communities. He grew spiritually during these days, gaining *"insight into his own heart and his spiritual necessities."*

Samuel was deeply concerned for the spiritual condition of everyone around him; he began to buy religious tracts and booklets to distribute. He said, *"I feel a great desire for the advancement of the cause of Christ. Have been much concerned for the salvation of my oldest brother. I have four sisters and three brothers all members of the church, excepting him. Wrote to him again the past week, on the subject of his soul's salvation; have sent him two tracts, 'Eternity,' and 'Leslie's Short Method;' the Lord bless them to his conversion. Procured two thousand three hundred and thirty-six pages of tracts, which I have been giving to the students and others."*

Samuel wondered if God might be calling him to be a church planter in some spiritually destitute part of Virginia, but God began to open his thinking to service as a foreign missionary. The importance of using his life wisely, especially for the spread of the Gospel, was becoming more powerful in his mind. He said, *"Wherever I am, or whatever I do, I will endeavor to do good. What an awfully solemn thing it is to live, seeing that something I say or do may be the means of saving or destroying a soul!"*

The Southern Baptist Convention was formed in May of 1845, just as Clopton was pondering the direction of his future ministry. Several pastors approached him with the possibility of his becoming a missionary because they felt he was an excellent candidate for such important service. James B. Taylor, who was close to Samuel during those days, remembered "the continual solicitude, which the investigation gave him. By day and night it constantly pressed upon his heart. At length he considered it a call of God. He could not resist the claim. After consulting his most judicious friends, and especially his Heavenly Father, he determined to offer himself to the board."

On September 1, 1845, the Board of Foreign Missions, after examining Samuel Clopton carefully, appointed him as the first Southern Baptist missionary. Two months later, they examined and appointed his close friend and college classmate, George Pearcy, as their second foreign missionary. Both men were thrilled and humbled by their appointments and delighted in the decision of the Board to send them together to serve in Southern China. George Pearcy wrote of his appointment, *"How little did I think, in all my course, that the Lord was raising me up for such a work as this! I had hoped, in process of time, to be prepared for places of usefulness, but I did not expect that the Lord would call me to a work so important. Who is sufficient for such a work? The Lord strengthen and help me, and make me useful."*

It was decided they would not leave for China immediately but would stay in the USA a few months longer. They attended medical lectures at the college and spoke in numerous churches. In a sweet providence of God, both young men found young women, who loved them *and* the missionary cause. Samuel married Keziah Turpin, daughter of Rev. Miles Turpin in April of 1846. George Pearcy married Frances Miller six weeks later. These four young people formed a close friendship that stands as a beautiful and enduring example of missionary families working together as a team.

June 15, 1846, is a very important date in the history of Southern Baptist missions. It was on that day that the Cloptons and Pearcys were publically designated as our missionaries. Their commissioning service at Second Baptist Church in Richmond was the first of what is today called a "sending celebration." This service had a profound impact on all present and was vital in establishing Southern Baptists as a functioning missionary people. Everyone was delighted and awed to have missionary J. Lewis Shuck and Chinese Christian evangelist Yong Seen Sang (Yeung Hing) speak during the service. In 1845, China had an estimated population of 400 million compared to less than 20 million in the United States. Yet, such overwhelming need was not intimidating to the small band of missionaries because the joy of obedience to Christ was their strength.

That night James B. Taylor gave the charge to our missionaries in his new role as the first Corresponding Secretary of the Foreign

Mission Board. Taylor began, "The great empire of China is to be
the field of your labors. You go out, not as ambassadors from an
earthly government, but as ministers of the kingdom of Christ, not
to treat with secular powers on great national questions, but to bear
communications of divine love, beseeching the heathen to be rec-
onciled to God. **Yours is an office unequaled in dignity by any
within the gift of man**. It has relation to the soul and eternity. The
responsibilities involved are of the most solemn character."

Taylor charged them to keep up regular correspondence with
the Board, to be diligent in maintaining good relationships within
the missionary team, to be careful and wise in their spending of
money, to mingle daily with the Chinese, and to acquire the language as soon as possible. Furthermore, he urged them to guard
themselves against despondency, to live pure lives, and to cultivate
their spirituality.

In addressing why they should endeavor to learn Chinese
quickly, Taylor said:

> As soon as you shall sufficiently acquire the lan-
> guage to make yourselves clearly understood, you
> are to engage in preaching the gospel. This is your
> appropriate work. For this you are distinctly sent
> forth; you go from this land not to engage in scien-
> tific research or pecuniary speculations, not to rep-
> resent the best form of government or to exhibit the
> various stores of human knowledge, but **to preach
> the gospel**. You can, indeed, show to them the
> purest system of ethics the world has ever seen, but
> this would only still more embitter the cup of their

misery were it not that you can point to the Lamb of God that taketh away the sin of the world. Hold up, then, the cross and know nothing among them but Jesus Christ, and him crucified. You may almost endlessly diversify your methods of teaching. Your arguments and illustrations may vary according to the character and circumstances of those you address, but in all places and at all times the love of God to a lost race is to be the great theme of your addresses.... When you begin to publish the salvation of the gospel, they may not receive your message—you may be treated with scorn by some and with opposition by others. Under such circumstances you will be in danger of yielding to discouragement. But you need not despond. By whose command do you go forth? Is it not the glorified Redeemer's? On whose promise do you rely for support? Is it not that of the immutable God? He who sends you to preach the gospel has said, 'Lo, I am with you alway, even to the end of the world.'

On the following day, they left Richmond for New York, and on June 22, 1846, they set sail for China aboard the ship *Cahota*. Taylor worked feverishly to help them buy all the needed supplies for their mission. He accompanied them to the ship, which he described as "a fine vessel, and the accommodations are ample. She has a cow on board for giving milk, several sheep and pigs for the use of the table, and about one thousand fowls, with all the luxuries of the season for present use, and an abundant supply of everything necessary for the comfort of the passengers."

The Hon. Alex H. Everett, the United States' official representative to China, was also a passenger on this first-class vessel. After a tender deck-side prayer service, Taylor bid them a father's farewell, and the ship cast off and quickly sailed away. They traveled south the entire length of the Americas around the dangerous waters of Cape Horn and into the Pacific Ocean. The *Cahota* arrived in Canton in November after a journey of more than four months!

They immediately set about finding a place to live and tutors to teach them the language. The Pearcys and the Cloptons got along well, but their living conditions were rough. Their house was located on a low-lying street between a tavern and a duck market. The stench was constantly overpowering. In an early example of missionary humor, they tell of running up to a nearby terrace to grab an occasional mouthful of fresh air.

Samuel worked diligently to learn the language and to understand the spiritual condition of the people. He wrote home, *"I had often thought this to be a great field of usefulness, before coming here, but I have to say, the one half had not been told me. What a mighty wilderness! What a moral waste! I look upon it with amazement and pity; and in view of all the difficulties in the way, I am almost compelled to exclaim with the prophet in his vision, 'Can these dry bones live?' Come, O thou Spirit of the Holy One, breathe upon these slain, that they may live."*

These early months were filled with important and exciting events. Samuel and Keziah celebrated the birth of a son, Samuel Cornelius Clopton Jr.—the first Southern Baptist MK (missionary kid). When disgruntled Chinese workers attacked and threatened to burn the British factories in which they worked, the missionaries were forced to evacuate. The British Navy responded by attacking Canton. Thousands of Chinese fled with their families. Samuel took the wives to Hong Kong while George stayed to protect the mission house. During this trip, Samuel had several opportunities to share the Gospel with crowds using a translator, but he longed to be able to converse freely in the Chinese language.

Only eight months after arriving in China, Ambassador Everett died and was buried. Samuel attended the funeral of his countryman and stood for hours in the exceedingly hot sun. He returned home, ill with a high fever and vomiting. About a week later, he said to Keziah, *"I trust in my Saviour, and love him more than ever. I would like to live longer, for your sake and the little boy's; and I would like to preach the gospel to these dying heathen, but I am resigned to my Saviour's will; if he calls me, I am ready to go live near to God."* On July 7, 1847, he passed into the presence of the Lord. He was only thirty-one years old. Our first missionary appointed was our first missionary to die—less than one year after his arrival on the field.

His wife and fellow missionaries were stunned. George Pearcy lamented:

> *So sudden and unexpected was the event, we can scarcely realize that he is gone. But every thing tells us that he has indeed left us. In the social circle and at the family altar we hear not that voice with which we were so delighted to mingle ours. His seat is vacant at the table; his study, now still and lonely. Our teachers and the disciples come in, and*

mournfully say, 'Clopton the teacher has quickly ascended to heaven.' All around are sad. Sister Clopton's heart is bleeding, and we are all bowed down as one that mourneth for his mother.

Keziah returned to America with her son, arriving ten months after her husband's death. Her return trip was vastly different from her outgoing voyage. Two years after her marriage to Samuel, she was now a widow and a single mother. Her missionary hopes were dashed. She then devoted herself to raising young Samuel. She refused an annuity from the Board for herself, but she accepted one for the boy. Historical records indicate that by 1859, when Samuel Jr. was twelve years old, Keziah had already died.

The death of missionary Samuel C. Clopton Sr. was a profound blow to everyone committed to the cause of Southern Baptist foreign missions. How could God permit this to happen? Does He not care if the unevangelized peoples of the earth hear His Gospel? Does He not protect his ambassadors? Missionary supporters decided to put their hands over their mouths and bow in humble submission to Almighty God. Truly, God's ways are not our ways. *His* mission will be accomplished in *His* way and in *His* time.

Clopton may have been the first Southern Baptist missionary to die on the field, but he certainly was not the last. Many have died in missionary service, and even more have permanently lost their physical, mental, and emotional health. **Samuel Clopton's early death forced Southern Baptists to count the cost and to realize Christ's mission will only be accomplished with great sacrifice**. We cannot be followers of "the man of sorrows" without taking up our own cross. The spread of the Gospel will cost us. People will die in this effort, but everyone dies. The question is not *what do we die from?* Rather, *what do we live for?*

Samuel Jr. lost both mother and father before he was a teenager, but he did not become bitter against the cause of Christ. He was converted and shortly after helped to start a Sunday school on Clay Street in Richmond; one of the classes was made up of Chinese immigrants! He was finally ordained to the ministry after struggling for years to complete his education. The Clay Street Mission blossomed into a church, known as Calvary Baptist, and Samuel Jr. became its first pastor, serving from 1877-1892. During his pastoral career, he trained many young men for the ministry. After leaving Calvary, he continued to serve as a pastor in several different congregations until his death in 1904 at the age of forty-seven.

One touching tribute to this only son of our first missionary was given by Mrs. John Pollard, who was a member of his congregation in Richmond. She was deaf but faithfully attended church each week. Every Sunday morning, as Samuel Jr. was getting ready to preach, he handed Mrs. Pollard the notes of his sermon. She said that the kindness of her pastor enabled her "to enjoy the services along with those who might hear the words from his lips. I do not know, but it seems to me not one pastor in a thousand would have thus pitied my infirmity. How tenderly I think of him today."

In addition, Samuel Jr. was known and loved by virtually every Chinese person in Richmond. What about foreign missions? Well, Samuel Jr. faithfully served on the Board as a manager (trustee) of foreign missions for fifteen years. Yes, he did serve behind the scenes, but like thousands of trustees across our missionary history, his service was absolutely vital.

The mission of saving sinners belongs to God. God does not promise that we will reach Heaven's shores unscathed by sickness, persecution, hardship, struggle, or death; He does promise we will arrive. And when we do, our earthly sufferings will not be worth comparing to our heavenly joys. Every tear wiped away. Every act of faithful service remembered and rewarded. What a day when we get to meet these faithful servants of Jesus Christ! Above all, what a day when we meet the Savior, who came to ransom a family from every nation, language, tribe, and tongue! **What a day**!

Samuel Clopton Jr. (1847-1905), son of the first Southern Baptist missionary

Chapter Three

CHARLES GAILLARD

d.o.b. unknown-1861
Tragedy Made Beautiful

"He has made everything beautiful in its time.
Also, he has put eternity into man's heart, yet so
that he cannot find out what God has done from
the beginning to the end."   **Ecclesiastes 3:11**

O n July 27, 1862, a typhoon of unprecedented violence blew over the city of Canton (Guangzhou) in Southern China. Some reports estimated that over 37,000 people lost their lives in that horrific storm. Ships and boats were strewn onto the banks of the Pearl River and into the surrounding fields. Houses creaked and collapsed in the ferocious winds. Among the dead was Charles Washington Gaillard. The timbers of his house fell, crushing him to death immediately. When he died, his wife Eva was only a few feet from him, watching as he tried to close a door that had blown open during the storm. Charles and Eva had been serving as Southern Baptist missionaries in China for eight years since 1854.

In 1861, fifteen months prior to his tragic death, Charles wrote to the Foreign Mission Board (SBC) saying, *"When I go to heaven*

I do not want to go alone, but to collect a whole army of this people to go with me." He had preached the Gospel thousands of times and had seen a small, but steady, stream of converts, especially in the last three or four years of his life. He would not, however, live long enough to see an army of Christians gathered. Yet, God's thoughts are not our thoughts, and God's ways are not our ways. God's ways and God's thoughts are higher, better, and more surprising than ours. He makes everything beautiful **in His time**.

The date of Charles Washington Gaillard's birth in South Carolina is uncertain; however, his *second birth* happened in 1848, in Starkville, Mississippi. In July of that year, he attended a revival service. He resolved not to return when he realized it was a *Baptist* meeting. In his words, *"I had been taught to have very little respect for that denomination."* His parents and all of his other relatives were Presbyterians, but his friends urged him to attend again, and so he did. On the third day he was under immense conviction, believing his case to be hopeless and his day of grace past. He said, *"I felt my utter inability to save myself—that my condemnation would be just. This frame of mind continued until sunset, at which time I again went to the grove and bowed in prayer. While there, I felt a change of mind, my hard heart was subdued to love and praise to God, who for Christ's sake had pardoned my sins. I felt as I had never felt before, and feelings which I cannot describe."*

Gaillard's next concern was which church he should join. He was very reluctant to join with the Baptists because he believed immersion to be unbiblical. Since none of his Presbyterian family was nearby for counsel, he said, *"I then took the Testament, and went into my room, and asked God to direct me in the way that I should go, and then began to read; and in a few days I was willing* to be united with the Baptists, which I did and was baptized by Bro. C. S. McCloud."

Within weeks, Gaillard was overwhelmed with a sense that it was his duty to preach the Gospel. He wrote, *"I tried to banish the thought from my mind, feeling that I was too ignorant and unworthy to engage in such a high calling. But this impression still remained and continued to gain strength, that I should preach, and that I should go to those who had not heard the gospel."* At the urging of Pastor McCloud, he attended Union University (then located in Murfreesboro, Tennessee) to study for the ministry, and he graduated in 1853.

In addition to Charles Gaillard, Union University was the training ground of other missionary pioneers, including T.P. Crawford (North China Mission) and W.D. Powell (Mexico Mission). While a student, Gaillard was the president of the Union University chapter of Phi Gamma Delta. He was ordained to the Gospel ministry by the First Baptist Church of Murfreesboro. In his application letter to the Foreign Mission Board, he concluded, *"I have but one object in view, the glory of God, and the salvation of the millions who are perishing for want of the bread of life."*

He married Eva Mills from New York, and they sailed to China in April of 1854, arriving four months later. Their field of service was Canton and the surrounding villages. Over the next eight years, they were forced to flee Canton on numerous occasions due to armed conflicts between the Chinese and various foreign powers. Each time they retreated to Macau where their young daughter, Helen Baptista Gaillard, died and was buried. Broken-hearted, Charles and Eva pressed on in their missionary service.

Above all, Charles Gaillard was a preacher. He acknowledged how difficult the Chinese language was to learn, but he was relentless in his efforts. He had an urgent, life or death message to proclaim, and the sooner he could communicate without a translator, the better. After several years of study, he lamented that his sermons only lasted forty-five minutes because he ran out of energy and words.

One of the most important strategies that Gaillard employed in spreading the Gospel was literature distribution. According to his annual report for 1856, he had distributed 32,200 copies of Testaments and tracts. Gaillard worked tirelessly, but he recognized that preaching the Gospel will not bring about true conversion unless the Holy Spirit does a sovereign work of grace in the hearts of the hearers. He said, *"We have proof every day that without the Spirit of God we cannot preach and the people cannot believe."*

Letters to Christians back home were filled with his pleas, *"Will not our brothers in America pray more earnestly for the conversion of these people?"* He urged not only prayers but repeatedly called for new missionaries saying, *"I wrote to you year before last, to try and send us ten single men. I wish that number were here now, prepared to preach to this people.... If merchants, for the sake of money, can come out single and remain here ten or fifteen years, which is longer than most missionaries stay, why can not missionaries come single, for the sake of the Gospel?"*

Canton was a vast field of labor in itself, but Gaillard pressed into the surrounding villages to preach and give out Gospel literature. Additionally, he journeyed 190 miles up the Pearl River into territory where no Protestant missionary had ever been. Gaillard, a handful of Chinese Christian evangelists, and missionary Rosewell

H. Graves were a whirlwind of Gospel-centered activity. He said that China would not be given to Christ as His inheritance until *"as much has been done for the spread of the gospel in China, as has been done and is still doing to effect the opium traffic, then will thousands of hearts and voices be raised in songs of praise to him who died to redeem a lost world. Oh, brethren, when shall that blessed day dawn on this dark land?"*

In 1860, after six lean years, Gaillard began to see a harvest. He wrote, *"As the result of our labors, we have baptized, on profession of their faith in Christ, 37 persons—16 of whom were females. Brother Graves has also baptized three English soldiers. The whole number of the church was 58."* He averaged one sermon every day, taught a six-month course on theology, and published his Chinese *Notes on the Acts of the Apostles* during the course of that year. He faithfully taught the church members that it was their duty to share the Gospel with family and friends. He trained them to be systematic and generous in the giving of their finances in order to build up the church. He reported, *"We contribute monthly; each member gives something, if it is only the fourth of a cent."* He summarized that banner year by saying, *"Our prospects for the further success of the gospel are as good as the promises of God are sure. The Spirit of the Lord has been with us all the year. We have had baptisms nearly every month...."*

Gaillard heard of the gathering storm clouds of war in the United States and the possibility that the Board might recall its missionaries. He could hardly bear the thought and appealed to the Board in these words:

*Our hope is in God. For myself, I entertain no idea
of leaving my work altogether. If necessity should
compel you to call home any of your missionaries,
I beg that I may be the last (though I may be the
least). If you can find the funds to give me three
hundred dollars salary, and one hundred and fifty
dollars house rent, I will remain at my post, as long
as the Lord will permit me. I desire to live and labor
here, at least twenty-five years longer, if it be the
will of the Lord. I have no desire, and therefore no
idea of seeing America again. I am as happy and
contented here as I could be anywhere this side of
heaven. And when I go to heaven, I do not want to
go alone, but to collect a whole army of people to
go with me. The Lord is still with us. I have baptized four converts since my last. Two of them are
women, our nurse, and the other an old lady seven-
ty-four years old.*

In his last years of service, Gaillard wrote of two young men
who had professed faith, *"If these two men become true and zealous
Christians, to labor in their own towns, I will be more than repaid
for all the sacrifice of a missionary life."* One of these young men
was described as being about fifteen or sixteen years of age. He had
been *"treated so badly by his adopted mother, that he had to leave.
He then hired himself to a barber who turned him off in a few days
because he would talk to the people about Jesus, when they came
to be shaved. He is very zealous for the cause of Christ and very
diligent in studying the Scriptures, as he goes out every Sunday*

and preaches, sometimes in the streets and sometimes in the poor-house...if he lives we have hope, that he will be a very useful man." His name was **Lough Fook**. Gaillard would not live to know the fascinating ministry of Lough Fook—but you will!

Even though Gaillard's earthly life ended beneath the timbers of his house, his labors continue to bear fruit long after his death. In a very unique way, the author of this book is part of that fruit-fulness. Praise God for the life and labors of Charles Washington Gaillard. Read on, and remember that God is weaving together the threads of our faithful service. His plans stretch far into the future beyond our wildest imagination!

Chapter Four

LOUGH FOOK

*c.*1841-1884

Morningstar of the Chinese Missionary Movement

"Have this mind among yourselves, which is yours
in Christ Jesus, who, though he was in the form
of God, did not count equality with God a thing
to be grasped but emptied himself, by taking the
form of a servant..."   **Philippians 2:5-6**a

In 1861, Lough Ah Fook "*sold himself as a pig*" to reach others
with the Gospel of Jesus Christ. Missionary Charles Gaillard
had baptized Lough a few years earlier. Lough had been an appren-
tice in a barbershop when he first heard of Jesus and believed in
his heart. He immediately began sharing his faith with his cus-
tomers. He asked the owner of the shop to deduct one-seventh of
his wages, so he could take Sundays off to attend worship services
and to devote himself to the Lord's work. The barber refused and
fired him.

Lough was adopted by his aunt, who raised him as her son.
When she heard that he had become a Christian, she was furious
and did everything she could to get Lough to turn away from his

newfound faith. She even hid his clothes and shoes, so he could not leave the house. To give Lough some relief from the incessant persecutions in Canton, Rosewell Graves took Lough with him on his countryside preaching tours.

Missionary Graves was deeply impressed by the young convert, who shared Christ everywhere they went. Lough refused financial help from the missionaries, preferring to pay his own way. He used his skills as a barber and occasionally hired himself out as a servant. Graves remarked, *"He was always cheerful and spent much time reading his Bible. He was distinguished by his strong common sense in all that he did."*

After a few years, Lough came to believe God was opening a door for him to reach his fellow Chinese for Christ by leaving China. The early 1860s was the height of the British labor recruitment in Southern China. After the emancipation of slaves throughout the British Empire, there was an urgent lack of laborers, especially in the sugarcane fields of the West Indies. This led to a new system of contracted laborers. Most of the recruits for this system were from India and a smaller portion from South China. The workers legally bound themselves for a term of service that lasted from five to seven years. They gradually paid back the cost of their government-subsidized emigration, and the remaining wages belonged to them. Those who entered this form of indentured servitude were called "coolies."

Most of the Chinese coolies in the early years were regarded as "the offscourings of Canton — gaol-birds, loafers and vagabonds." These men quickly deserted the plantations and lived on the fringes, engaging in "bootlegging, burglary and robbery and kept brothels and gambling houses." As the system developed, the quality of the immigrants began to rise. Many of the later Chinese coolies left Canton due to racial and political conflict and because of the lack of adequate job opportunities.

Lough saw indentured servitude as an open door for the Gospel, which allowed him to evangelize his own people in a foreign land. Rosewell Graves later said, *"He told me he thought it would be a favorable opportunity to influence them, as they would be removed from their idolatrous influences which surrounded them in China, and, at the same time, as strangers in a strange land, would feel the need of the comfort which religion brings. So he determined to cast in his lot with them, that he might preach to them. He, therefore, engaged himself to go as a coolie—'sold himself as a pig,' as the Chinese call it—and went to work as a laborer on a plantation."*

According to Graves, Lough's contract as a coolie was to last for seven years. On his voyage to the South American cane fields of Demerara (British Guiana), Lough shared his faith with his fellow immigrants, and several professed faith in Jesus. Upon their arrival in Demerara, Lough maintained his relationship with the new converts. He began Sunday worship services and other Christian meetings on weeknights. As God prospered his efforts, more people trusted in Christ. Christian friends in British Guiana were so impressed with Lough's efforts that they bought out the final years of his contract, so he could devote himself to evangelization and church planting. He became closely connected with Brethren missionaries sent out under the ministry of George Müller in England.

Lough was set apart for the ministry—presumably by the Brethren missionaries—and soon began to baptize converts. They formed the first Baptist Church in British Guiana at Peter's Hall,

East Bank, Demerara. **It appears that this church, which was planted in 1861 or 1862, is the first Baptist church not only in British Guiana, but also in all of South America.** A second church was founded at Leonora in the West Coast of Demerara. These first two congregations soon planted two others—one at Camuni Creek and the other at Bagotsville.

These four churches and their members were not examples of "easy-believism." They were well-ordered congregations that clearly set forth biblical expectations for their members. Lough maintained a life-long correspondence with Rosewell Graves in Canton. Graves says of Lough, *"He was a decided Baptist in all his convictions and had the courage of his convictions at all times. In one of his letters he told me he had been studying the Greek New Testament for himself, and was more firmly persuaded than ever of the soundness of our position. In discipline he was strict, and his church resembled the old Baptist churches in this respect."*

Members were taught the importance of holy living and were disciplined for serious sin. They were expected to abstain from work on the Lord's Day and to be in attendance at worship services. They were taught to tithe and to give generously to missions. Each member was encouraged to be a personal witness for Jesus Christ and to share the Gospel with people in their daily lives. Before 1920, the ministry was carried out in Chinese (Cantonese); after 1920, they no longer needed a Chinese-speaking pastor because everyone spoke English.

A vital part of Lough's ministry was training leaders and pastors. One young man, Tso Sune, returned to Canton where he served as a pastor, and he was highly regarded by the missionaries. Graves says Pastor Sune *"served as the efficient pastor at different times of*

44

our three principal churches in Canton, Shiu Hing and Tsing Yuen."
Graves never ceased to be amazed at how the far-flung work among Chinese in South America came back to bless China in so many ways.

Lough Fook's ministry was most unique in the area of financial support for missions. Graves described the work of the Chinese Baptists in British Guiana:

> *They have three chapels and four houses—two of the latter used as parsonages, and the other two rented out. There are three stores, the profits of which are devoted to mission work. The proceeds of trade in two of them, called "Success through Grace," and "Added Success through Grace," are devoted to the Foreign Mission work; while the proceeds of the other, called "Additional Success through Grace," are appropriated to their Home Mission work in Guiana. They have a flourishing missionary society of sixty members, each of whom pay twenty-five cents per month into the treasury.*

The Chinese Baptists regularly sent money back to China to aid the Christian work in their native land. Moreover, they sent missionaries to the interior of British Guiana to reach the Amerindians for Christ, establishing a Baptist church in the town of Lethem. When Lough Fook died in 1884, there were two hundred members in the churches he had planted, and they contributed more than $2,000 annually to missions. At that point, there were *only* a total of 3,000 Chinese in British Guiana!

Chinese success in British Guiana led many to return to China or to move on to greater opportunities in other countries. By 1932, all of the Chinese Baptist churches had closed or joined with the Brethren denomination. Yet, in the seventy years of their existence the Chinese Baptists had done an invaluable work that foreshadowed the future of missions as *from everywhere to everywhere*.

Lough Fook was about forty-three years old when he took his last breath on May 15, 1884. He had been suffering from *"pulmonary consumption and hemorrhages from the lungs for some time past."* We do not know anything about Lough's wife except that she must have preceded him in death. At Lough's death, their two daughters were left in the care of the wife of an English missionary.

Lough Fook is one of those seeds that dies and falls unseen and unknown into the ground; yet, Graves says of him, *"Such a man has not lived in vain. Though dying at an early age—about 43, I think—he has made his mark on all times and left behind an example for all time. He is a proof of what the grace of God can do for a Chinaman and what a Chinaman can do when renewed by the grace of God. May his mantle fall upon others of his race. The useful life and happy death of this dear brother should lead us to labor more earnestly for the conversion of the Chinese."*

Lough Fook came to faith through the ministry of Charles Gaillard. He took the form of a servant and carried the Gospel and the Baptist faith to South America. Even though the churches he planted do not remain, the root of his work was yet to bear much fruit.

Bradys leave for Guyana in 1962

Chapter Five

OTIS BRADY

1927-2002
Church Planter in Caribbean Lands

"Oh, magnify the LORD with me, and let us exalt
his name together!"   **Psalm 34:3**

**Letter from Otis W. Brady to Dr. Frank K. Means (FMB)
October 16, 1963:**

"*B*y some act of mercy, for many years Southern Baptists have
been on the approved list of churches in British Guiana.
*This is the list approved by the Governor in Council. We are number
32 on the list and listed as the Southern Baptist Church, U.S.A....
The only possible way I see for accounting for this listing comes
from the Chinese Baptists who once were here. As you know they
were a part of our missionary work in China. Though the group has
long since died out the listing may have come from them.*"

"*By some act of mercy...*" are the words with which missionary
Otis Brady began his amazed explanation of how Southern Baptists
were given legal standing to stay and plant churches in British

Guiana. Charles Gaillard and Lough Fook were not names that
Otis Brady knew; yet, these men were a part of a complex and
beautiful tapestry that God had been weaving for more than one
hundred years. The ministry of Lough Fook provided the open door
for Southern Baptists to enter British Guiana and to begin working
there on the eve of the nation's independence from England.
Guyana, as it would be known after independence in 1966, was
ripe for the Gospel message during those tumultuous years. God's
timing is perfect!

On August 1, 1962, the Brady family's flight arrived in
British Guiana to an animated crowd of more than three thousand
Guyanese. Actually, the crowd had gathered to express support for
another passenger on the same plane, Premier Cheddi Jagan. Jagan
was returning from New York where he had appealed to the UN,
pressing for Guyanese independence from Great Britain. Britishers,
Americans, and especially missionaries were largely *persona non
grata* during those days. The British Guiana to which the Bradys
arrived was a powder keg of political, racial, and religious tensions. Communism was making major inroads; this alarmed both
the British and American governments and delayed independence.

The Bradys followed the motorcade of the Premier into
Georgetown, the capital. Otis says of that journey:

> *This 28-mile trip from the Air Port afforded us a*
> *good opportunity to observe the people as they lined*
> *the road to see the Premier. Our primary interest*
> *was the people, but we also looked at the Hindu*
> *temples, Moslem mosques, prayer flags, Christian*
> *churches, houses built on stilts, drainage ditches and*

canals, sugar cane estates, lovely tropical flowers, and many animals. A roadside sign had these words on it: "THERE IS ONE GOD. MUHAMED IS HIS LAST PROPHET." It was not difficult for us to realize that we were in a different country. All of this gave us a new sense of the presence and guidance of the living Lord. We have an abiding sense of satisfaction in being where He wants us to be.... As we observe the subtle, and often not so subtle, cries for allegiance coming from so many directions to the people, we find an added sense of responsibility in **sharing the unsearchable riches of God in Christ.**

The door to Guyana remained open to the Bradys for the next fourteen years. During that time, many people were converted to Jesus Christ, dozens of churches were planted, leaders were trained, and a Christian bookstore and a camp were initiated. The Bradys started the first congregation, Central Baptist Church, in their home. It served as the fellowship hub for the other Baptist churches that soon emerged. Otis describes the beginning of Central, *"Sunday morning we had the roll call of charter members and as they individually answered the roll by "Saved by Grace" there came a real sense of the significance of the occasion of constituting the church. Then the thirty-five charter members (28 by baptism) stood and made covenant together with God by reading the church covenant and the prayer of dedication."* They sang, "In Christ There is No East or West." As he looked at the faces of this new congregation, Otis was overwhelmed with the living testimony to the power of God to save people of every skin-color, ethnicity, and background, bringing them into one Body. The truth of the hymn was brightly painted in the scene of the room, "Join hands, then, brothers of the faith, What-e'er your race may be: Who serves my Father as a son is surely kin to me."

Otis Brady was an unlikely person to be ministering in such a diverse cultural setting. He was born October 15, 1927, on a farm in rural upstate South Carolina. He was the twelfth of thirteen children born to Otis and Lizzie Brady. Otis Sr. was a farmer, who fell on hard times during the depression years of the 1930s and ultimately, lost the farm he loved. He turned to alcohol as a refuge during those bleak years. The painful memories, resulting from his father's drunkenness, produced emotional scars that Otis Jr. would bear the rest of his life.

Otis had a deep appreciation for nature from his earliest days. He said, *"I always enjoyed the outdoors. As I looked at the beauty of nature—the sun, moon, and stars—I would think of the powerful God who created all of this. There was never a time when I doubted that God existed, but I did not have a personal relationship with Him."* When a little church near the farm started a Sunday school for children, Otis began to learn more about Jesus. He commented, *"I understood the life and resurrection of Jesus in a deeper way. I responded to Jesus and asked him to forgive me of my sins and live in my heart."*

Soon after his conversion, a missionary to China visited their church. She illustrated the Gospel on a flannel graph with a picture of earth and heaven separated by a huge gulf. As people came to the end of their lives, they fell off the earth into hell because of the great distance between them and God in heaven. That gulf was created by our sin. Next, the missionary put a cross between earth and heaven and showed people walking *on* the cross of Christ to eternal life. This simple Gospel illustration revolutionized Otis' understanding. His own sense of trust in Jesus was deepened, and he became aware of the untold millions of people headed to hell, having never heard of the Savior, Jesus Christ. At that moment Otis Brady, as an eight-year-old boy, was called to be a missionary! Many circumstances in his life would change, but that strong, clear sense that God had called him to be a missionary remained.

In 1939, when Otis was twelve, his father died as result of injuries sustained in an auto accident. His father had been emotionally distant for years due to his increasing drunkenness, but now he was completely gone. Otis Jr. experienced the loss deeply and felt "fatherless." However, at church he learned about *"God the Father who was perfect in all his ways and that he was one of his sons."* According to Otis, knowing this reality began a healing process that helped him, in many ways, overcome the tragic failures of his earthly father. In fact, this was a blessing in disguise as one of Otis Brady's greatest contributions was being a "spiritual father" to many "fatherless" young believers on the mission field.

When Otis was a teenager, the Bradys lived in the town of Duncan, South Carolina. Otis worked at the local mill after school to help support his widowed mother during the hard times of the Second World War. His older brother Harold, serving in the US Army, was killed by the Germans during the Allied invasion of Italy. Otis missed his brother terribly, and Harold's death had a lasting impact him. When Otis graduated from high school, he joined the Air Force as the war was coming to an end. While Otis was serving in Panama, he took every available opportunity to help the missionaries, and this confirmed his calling and desire *"to make Christ known wherever I may be."*

After completing his tour of duty, Otis set out to complete a college degree, which seemed virtually impossible for a young man from his impoverished roots. Thankfully, the GI Bill opened the door to higher education. He attended Furman University in Greenville, South Carolina, which was one of the main Baptist colleges in the state at that time. He was shocked to find that his first roommate was German. This was a test. Would he pre-judge this young man? Would he hate him for what the Germans had done to his brother? God won the victory in his heart; Otis released his bitterness.

This not only made it possible for him to be friends with this young man, but it set him firmly on the road to love everyone he met—no matter their background, skin-color, or religion. Otis majored in history and making friends. He was quite popular, and it seemed he went out on dates with most of the girls on campus. But nothing could get his eyes off the mission field! After college he attended Southeastern Seminary in Wake Forest, NC. He also pastored Ellerbe Baptist Church on the weekends (His elder son John would pastor the same church many years later). He enjoyed his time at seminary and did well, but his heart was already on the mission field.

About that time, one of the most significant events in his life took place. A seminary classmate, John Clyde Yates Jr., introduced Otis to his younger sister, a student at Wake Forest College, which shared the campus with Southeastern Seminary. Clyde warned his sister that Otis had dated just about everybody and had even been engaged. Yet, this meeting of Otis and Martha blossomed. Very quickly, Otis asked Martha the burning question of the hour, *"Is God calling you to be a missionary?"* Otis really liked her, but he had to know if they were headed in the same direction.

Many people believe God is calling them into missions, but they marry someone with a different heart, and their calling never becomes a reality. Not so for Otis or Martha. God had given both of them a heart for the nations and a heart for each other. Otis proposed to Martha in the Rose Garden of nearby Duke University. Martha's father, Pastor John Clyde Yates Sr., officiated their marriage on August 7, 1954, in Charlotte, NC. While Otis finished seminary, they served Calvary Baptist Church in Roanoke Rapids, NC, where their first child, John Thomas Brady, was born.

Otis felt called to Africa—the Dark Continent—great need, far away, mysterious, and difficult... God called them to suffer for Jesus in the Bahamas, barely off the coast of Florida. The Bahamas was a significant leverage point because of immigration from all over the Caribbean. In 1956, they began a six-year ministry at the Bahamas Baptist Institute. Otis taught Bible, theology, and ministry-related classes while Martha taught English composition. The Institute drew students from across the English-speaking Caribbean. It was here they grew to love Caribbean peoples in all their glorious diversity. While the Bradys were living in the Bahamas, their second child, Martha Lynn, was born.

In March and April of 1961, three leaders of the Foreign Mission Board (SBC), Charles Bryan, Frank K. Means, and Baker James Cauthen, surveyed the Caribbean on a twenty-two day trip. This whirlwind tour confirmed the great need for Christ across the Caribbean. There were many Christian churches, but not much emphasis was placed on having a personal relationship with God through Jesus Christ. As Cauthen toured British Guiana, one of the largest and most racially diverse nations in the Caribbean, he was heard to say, "If I were younger, I'd plant my life here." The Bradys were invited to take the post, and after prayerful consideration, they did.

By the end of fourteen years of missionary service in Guyana, the work had grown tremendously. Numerous dramatic conversions, including many Hindus to Christ, were evidences of the Gospel's incredible power to save. One story is told of a young schoolteacher, who came to see Otis from the village of Maria's Pleasure. The teacher was not a Christian, but he had heard of Otis' ministry. For years he had been hungry for soul-satisfying truth, even to the point of visiting forty medicine men in search of answers and peace, but to no avail. Otis shared the Gospel, and the man *"gave his heart to the Lord in a trembling way."* He returned home and made official his common-law marriage, began witnessing to his family and neighbors, and became a faithful follower of Jesus Christ. By God's grace, experiences like this occurred over and over again. Otis graphically likened these conversions to Christ as a *"stepping out of midnight darkness."*

Baptist churches dotted the Guyanese landscape. The Bradys' youngest child, David, was born in Guyana in 1968. However, the political tensions continued throughout their ministry. Otis was falsely accused, as were many missionaries, of being a spy for the CIA. While on furlough in Landrum, SC, in 1975, they received word that their visas would not be renewed. They were not allowed to return to Guyana to get their belongings or to say goodbye to their many Guyanese brothers and sisters in Christ.

At that time, Otis was in his late forties and had already served for twenty years as a missionary. What would they do now that the door to Guyana had closed? Quit or start over from scratch? Southern Baptists were interested in beginning a new work in the Caribbean. This time the Board wanted to open work in Belize, the only English-speaking nation in Central America. Belize was a British Colony as Guyana had been. Curiously, records show that Southern Baptists first considered work in Belize in the 1850s among the Maya, but they did not follow through on that idea. Finally, Southern Baptists were ready to enter Belize in its closing years as a British Colony.

Traveling to Belize was very different from traveling to Guyana. In the summer of 1976, the bicentennial of US independence, the Bradys left South Carolina on their journey to Belize. Their mode of transportation was a Ford Mercury Bobcat station wagon. If they had driven directly to Belize, the trip would have been about 2,600 miles long. However, they detoured to Guadalajara, Mexico, to study Spanish for one year. Even though English is the official language of Belize, a large percentage of people speak Spanish. Finally, on June 15, 1977, the Bradys drove their Bobcat from Chetumal, Mexico, across the border into Belize.

Their arrival began a ministry of almost nineteen years in this Caribbean nation, which is located in the heart of Central America. British Baptists had entered Belize in 1822, and Conservative Baptists entered the country in 1961. The Bradys worked closely with these groups to create a single, unified Belizean Baptist witness. The first church they planted in Belize City was on Kraal Road, an impoverished and under-served area. The only religious meeting place on that road was a Muslim mosque. As the

Bradys drove into the neighborhood for the first time, the sight of two Belizean women viciously attacking each other stopped them. Children quickly surrounded the women, shouting, "Kill ah, Kill ah."

Otis and Martha looked at each other and said, *"This is it."*

Young David asked, "This is what?"

They said, *"This is where God wants us to plant a church."*

The only structure large enough to house a church on Kraal Road was the Muslim mosque. The Bradys began to pray and asked others to do the same. Within weeks, the bank foreclosed on the mosque, and the building was put up for auction. On faith, Otis bid on the property. When his bid won, the only thing Otis lacked was the money. Gratefully, the First Baptist Church of Columbus, Georgia, stepped up to the challenge and sent the money to buy the building. At the last possible hour, the money arrived in miraculous fashion.

The Bradys prayed for the spiritual cleansing of the building and set in motion Calvary Baptist Church. The rough and violent neighborhood began to change, slowly but surely, by the power of the Gospel. A woman, who lived near the church, had taught children to gamble away their lunch money. She gave up that evil practice when she became a Christian. Her own children, who had been neglected, were clothed, fed, and converted. Calvary trained dozens of pastors and other ministry leaders, who were intentionally sent out to plant churches around the city and country.

The Bradys started church after church and trained many leaders. With the help of thousands of volunteers from the USA, church buildings were constructed across the country during those years. Many of the young Belizean converts continued on as faithful

Christians, but others fell by the wayside. Otis and Martha Brady pressed on.

Otis Brady was uniquely gifted to see leadership potential in young Christians *before* they could see it in themselves. He was always ready to take a *"calculated risk"* on them and to train them on the job. They all learned his axioms or "Otis-cisms." His most famous saying was, *"Be ready, to preach, pray or die at any moment."* Otis helped many a young leader put the *"preach and pray"* into practice.

Finally in 1996, Otis and Martha retired after forty years of missionary service. Otis was exhausted, overworked, and worn out. They returned to Landrum, South Carolina, and for one year, Otis recuperated. After that healing year, his strength returned. At sixty-nine years of age, he accepted a three-year assignment as a church-planting trainer. He traveled across the Caribbean to encourage missionaries in the task that had been at the heart of his ministry—church planting. When that assignment ended, he served three congregations in Polk County, NC, as interim pastor. He was even ordained as a deacon in his home church, Landrum First Baptist.

In 2002, six years after leaving Belize, Otis and Martha accepted a new assignment with the International Mission Board. With excitement, they anticipated being a part of the effort to plant a new church among the Druze people in Nazareth, Israel. That old pioneer flame was rekindled in Otis, with Martha enthusiastically by his side. They were scheduled to leave for Israel in March of that year. On Sunday, January 13, Otis supplied the pulpit at Landrum First Baptist. On Monday, he led a Bible study for his neighbors. On Tuesday, January 15, Martha left home for therapy on her injured hand. When she returned several hours later, fire trucks and emergency vehicles were parked in the driveway. A volunteer fireman, who was also a deacon at their church, gently held her saying, "Miss Martha, he's gone."

Otis had been burning leaves in the backyard. It was a windy day, and the fire got out of control. Apparently, he rushed out of the house to extinguish the fire. His heart gave out. The fire scorched his body, and he was gone. The news of his death was a blow to us all; yet, the man who taught us to be ready to preach, pray, or die at any moment—*was*. He *was* prepared. He *was* ready. His trust was not in his accomplishments as a missionary, but his faith was firmly and fully in Jesus Christ. He had preached Christ across the Caribbean, and he died trusting the Christ he had preached.

His body fell to the ground seventy-eight miles from where Charles Gaillard had first seen the light of day some **170 years before.** Both were born on the soil of South Carolina, and both were called to serve the King of Heaven and Earth—their lives and ministries linked by an Unseen Hand that is weaving together a family from every corner of the world. Nothing we do for Christ is ever in vain. We may not have the vision to see it, but our labors for the Lord *will* produce fruit long beyond the span of our earthly sojourn. Let us press on in faith, encouraged by Otis Brady's life verse, 1 Corinthians 15:58, *"Therefore, my beloved brothers, be steadfast, immovable, always abounding in the work of the Lord, knowing that in the Lord your labor is not in vain."*

Otis W. Brady Jr.

Guyana in the 1960s

Stabroek Market in Georgetown, Guyana, in the 1960s

Otis, Martha, David, and Jennifer in Belize in the 1980s

John Day Jr., missionary to Liberia

Chapter Six

JOHN DAY

1797-1859
Pioneer African-American Baptist Missionary
to Liberia

"Princes shall come out of Egypt; Ethiopia shall
soon stretch out her hands unto God." **Psalm 68:31**

Rev. John Day Jr. mounted the pulpit of Providence Baptist
Church in Monrovia, Liberia, on the first Sunday of February
in 1859. He was in his early sixties, a ripe old age for that time and
place. Providence Baptist Church was the oldest Baptist Church in
Africa. It began in 1822 with seven members, who had just landed
as colonists from the USA. Interestingly, they had covenanted
together as a church prior to leaving Richmond, Virginia, the year
before—making Richmond the place where the first Baptist Church
in Africa was founded. A former slave named Lott Cary was the
leader of the group and the first pastor of Providence church. They
were sent out under the auspices of the American Colonization
Society (ACS), which was formed with the idea of helping freed
slaves "return" to Africa to form a new society, filled with the blessings of evangelical Christianity but free from the ills of slavery.

This experiment in nation making had experienced many overwhelming difficulties, but Liberia had finally reached the status of an independent republic. A hymn written for the occasion of independence states clearly their dependence upon God and their desire to be a witness for Christ to all of Africa:

> May this young Republic be,
> Mindful of her trust in Thee.
> Bless, preserve, and her defend,
> Knowledge, skill, and virtue send;
> Let from her the gospel light
> Pierce the gloom of Afric's night.

John Day was not a member of the original group of colonists; however, he arrived in 1831, and quickly established himself as a leader in the community. He was known for the depth of his faith in Christ, the quality of his character, and the penetrating sharpness of his intellect. It was appropriate that the church he pastored was named Providence because Day's life was a beautiful illustration of the providential, guiding hand of God—a hand that rules and overrules in the affairs of men—ultimately, *"working all things according to the counsel of His will."*

Day had accomplished much in his almost thirty years in Liberia and had been active in many facets of the nation's political life. He was one of twelve men who signed the Liberian Declaration of Independence and Constitution, and he served both as lieutenant governor and as the second Supreme Court justice of the nation. He was self-taught in the science and art of jurisprudence and was noted for the wisdom of his decisions. Day also studied medical books and became quite proficient as a doctor. As significant as these accomplishments were, Day was—first and foremost—an ambassador for Christ.

Day was a missionary during most of his time in Liberia and for the last thirteen years of his life, a Southern Baptist missionary. In fact, he was the superintendent of all of our "colored" missionaries in Liberia and Sierra Leone. This is a chapter of Southern Baptist missions' history that is not well known, but should be. How did God guide John Day, an African-American, to become a missionary of a denomination that *had just been founded* upon a defense of the institution of slavery? Surely, God works in mysterious ways His wonders to perform.

John Day Jr. was born in 1797, in what is now called Emporia, Virginia. He was born into a family of free blacks in the time of slavery. His mother's family was a wealthy, land-owning family of free blacks. His father, John Day Sr., was the child of a white plantation owner's daughter, who conceived him through relations with her black carriage driver. She was sent away during her pregnancy to the secluded area of the Forks of the Yadkin in North Carolina. After delivering her son, she gave him to the Quaker family with whom she had stayed during the pregnancy, along with money to help educate little John.

As an adult, John Day Sr. was a cabinetmaker, and he lived in Virginia. John Day Sr. and his wife, Mourning Stewart Day, had two sons, John Jr. and Thomas. Both boys received a good education with the white children of their community. John Day Sr. was a skilled craftsman but, sadly, gave in to the vice of drunkenness and accumulated many financial debts. He left Virginia for North Carolina, seeking a fresh start. This unfortunate turn was still under the hand of God because it opened the door for both of his boys to move farther into North Carolina to Caswell County near Danville, Virginia.

In the town of Milton, John Jr. and Thomas opened a cabinet making business of their own. John left Milton and the new business after only a few years, but Thomas continued that business for the rest of his life. Thomas Day became one of the most sought-after furniture makers in all of North Carolina. The wealthy and elite of the state commissioned him to make his extraordinary pieces of furniture! Today, his pieces are even more highly valued, and Thomas Day is a legend of North Carolina craftsmanship.

John Day had become a Christian just a few years before moving to Milton, and there he found his teacher and discipler, Rev. Abner Clopton. Rev. Clopton had a profound impact on John and poured much learning and piety into the young man over the course of several years. Rev. Clopton also discipled James B. Taylor and Jeremiah Jeter, who both became pastors that were highly influential in the history of the Foreign Mission Board. Rev. Clopton introduced John Day to Luther Rice, who opened Day's mind to consider becoming a foreign missionary. Clopton is one of those men that the world barely knows, and hardly remembers, but his influence is beyond calculation.

Day applied to become a missionary to Haiti but was not appointed. After this devastating blow, he moved back to Virginia where he became involved with the American Colonization Society. Day, along with his wife and four children, immigrated to Liberia in 1831. When the family arrived in Africa, Day set up a cabinet making business to provide for their support. It is written of John Day:

He had not been long in the land, before he saw his companion stricken down by the relentless hand of death—a companion to whose charms and loveliness he was most keenly alive, and around whom the most ardent affections of his soul were so firmly entwined that the great deeps of his heart seemed upheaved by the severance. Then, one after another, he saw his beloved offspring wrapped in the chilling embraces of death, and conveyed to the house appointed for all living, until his whole family melted away from him, and none was left to remind him of the scenes and associations of the past. There he stood all-alone, in a new country, amid new scenes and associations. There he stood, like some solitary oak in the midst of winter, stripped of its foliage, and exposed, dry and defenseless, to all the pelting of the northern storms.

John experienced deep grief and depression for a number of years after the death of his family, but he refused to abandon his post. About five years later, the Triennial Baptist Convention hired Day as a part-time missionary. That convention was made up of Baptists in the North and South of the United States. It was that convention from which Southern Baptists would split over slavery in 1845. When that split took place, the new Southern Baptist Convention set its sights on two mission fields: China and Africa. In October of 1846, the board appointed two men already living in Liberia as missionaries, hoping they would accept. One was Alexander L. Jones and the other, John Day. When the news of their appointments arrived, Jones had just died, but **John Day accepted the appointment and became our first missionary to serve in Africa**.

During his thirteen years of service as a Southern Baptist missionary, Day was involved in many endeavors. He traveled throughout the country, preaching and planting churches. He also started two schools, and he was the supervisor of all our workers in Liberia and served as a "Baptist bishop" of sorts. He was completely committed to faithful proclamation of the Gospel of Jesus Christ as the focus of his ministry and the only hope for Africa. He wrote, *"To thousands I have shown that they are dead—that they cannot help themselves; but help in the living God alone is found. I preached to them of Jesus—his most endearing love—his righteousness, his atoning blood—his resurrection—his ascension into heaven, and his intercessions there."*

He was often very discouraged because of the slow response of the people to Christ and the Gospel. He said, *"We preach, they seem to listen, but cannot hear. God alone must unstop their deafened ears."* Day told of preaching in a small village:

> *I preached from the words, 'Except ye repent, ye shall all likewise perish.' I spoke of* **repentance** *as originating in a firm belief of God: his goodness, his forbearance, his love, and mercy.* **Its nature**: *sorrow for sin, shame of sin, hatred of sin, turning from sin.* **Its effects**: *softens the heart; humbles the mind; produces prayer; submission to God; brings peace to the soul.* **The consequence of not repenting**: *the heart is hardened; the affections*

*turned from God; God offended; conscience trou-
bled; death made dreadful; and in another world
leads to death that never dies—misery that never
ends. Closed by begging them to repent and turn to
God. He is now willing, ready and waiting to save
you. The poor man sat and stared me in the face, as
if he thought me deranged.*

Day had times of encouragement intermingled with the many frustrations. What sustained him through it all was the promise of God in Psalm 68:31, *"Ethiopia shall soon stretch out her hands unto God."* He saw "Ethiopia" as standing for Africa and all of its population. He believed God *could* and *would* turn the hearts of the unbelieving masses across that continent to Himself in faith. Surely, Day would be amazed at the growth of Christianity in Sub-Saharan Africa today! Between 1900 and 2010 the number of Christians has soared "almost 70-fold from about 7 million to 470 million. Sub-Saharan Africa now is home to about one-in-five of all the Christians in the world (21%)." John Day was certainly right to walk by faith and not by sight.

Day remarried and had at least two boys, but little is known of that family. He did not confine himself to living with the American immigrants but had a heart to reach the native Africans, especially the Bassa people, among whom he lived and worked for many years. In the final years of his life, John did move to the capital, Monrovia, where he became pastor of Providence Baptist Church. Additionally, he opened a school primarily for native African children and called it Day's Hope. What a beautiful name! It exemplified Day's undying hope in God's saving power towards Africa.

When John entered the pulpit on February 6, 1859, he did not know that he would be unable to preach that day. It is recorded, "When he arose to announce his text, he was seized with such weakness as rendered him wholly unable to proceed. Having been taken home, he went to bed, but from that bed he rose no more. On February 15, his spirit was summoned to eternal realities. The last assembly he met on earth was an assembly of God's people."

Let us hear once more Day's passion for the evangelization of Africa:

> *The earth does not afford a better scope for the display of goodness, love, mercy, and power, than does the colored race. And will God lose this chance of getting to himself glory? He raiseth the poor out of the dust, sets them among princes, and makes them inherit a throne of glory. My conclusion is, that as long as I live I will contribute to the accomplishment of this great object, the salvation of Africa. I feel it an object so near my heart, so connected with God's glory, that I apply the promise, those who bless Africa, God will bless, and those who curse Africa, God will curse. Feeling that I am engaged in a work adapted to secure the greatest glory to God, what a privilege I esteem it! How unwilling to abandon it! The redemption of heathen anywhere is a great work – a work worthy the people of God. But Africa is a land that God loves, has special promises, has been suffered to come exceedingly low, that the greater glory might redound to God,*

*who will redeem and exult her. Who that loves God
would not love Africa? Who that has felt his love,
would not desire to promote his glory? In what will
God be more glorified, than the evangelization of
Africa? O, brethren, come to this work.*

Day's life is a vital link in God's chain of witnesses to reach
the entire world with the Gospel of Jesus Christ. The story of John
Day and the other black missionaries in Liberia and Sierra Leone is
a little known, but fascinating, chapter in Southern Baptist history.
In a denomination deeply stained by the sin of slavery, Day's life
and witness bring hope that even the remaining stains of slavery
and racism can be fully cleansed on the level ground at the foot of
the cross. His legacy demonstrates the power of the Gospel to bring
people into one family, united with a common mission. Prayerfully,
Southern Baptists will have a brighter future where all races come
together in Christ to fulfill His Great Commission.

Thomas and Laurenna Bowen, missionaries to Nigeria

Chapter Seven

Thomas Jefferson Bowen

1814-1874
The David Livingstone of Southern Baptists

"By faith he went to live in the land of promise, as in
a foreign land, living in tents with Isaac and Jacob,
heirs with him of the same promise." **Hebrews 11:9**

Thomas Jefferson Bowen is one of the most remarkable missionary pioneers in Southern Baptist history. He has numerous
similarities to the well-known missionary, David Livingstone.
Unlike Livingstone, Bowen is largely unknown, even by his own
denomination. He was the first Southern Baptist missionary in its
two most fruitful fields: Nigeria (Yoruba) and Brazil. He was a
noted explorer, ethnographer, and linguist. He preached widely and
introduced many to the Gospel of Jesus Christ. Bowen's sweeping
vision for the work in Africa has guided subsequent generations of
missionaries.

Why is he largely forgotten? Well, his life ended sadly. He was
forced back to America by illness, not only of the body, but also
of the mind. His mental illness was exacerbated by dependence on
painkillers. He received very little understanding and compassion,

yet his story is vital. We must remember his incredible accomplishments, but we must look squarely at his struggles. Why? Illness — physical and mental — is a frequent cost of missionary service. We need to pray more fervently for the wellbeing of our missionaries and be more compassionate toward them when they experience breakdowns in their physical and mental health. Bowen's wife, Lurenna, bore the brunt of the public rejection of her husband. She said of those painful years, *"It was a sad and heavy affliction, worse than death."*

Thomas Jefferson Bowen was born on January 2, 1814, in Jackson County, Georgia. He was a born warrior. He fought in the Second Creek War in 1836. He and a fellow soldier were caught in an ambush. His friend was shot eight times and died. Bowen escaped with only one bullet wound. This close encounter with death did not deter him from a soldier's life but propelled him forward. He journeyed to Texas to fight for its independence from Mexico. Bowen joined the Texas Rangers in 1837 and was surprised when he was quickly commissioned as an officer. He fought in numerous battles over an eighteen-month period and distinguished himself for valor and leadership.

During the war for Texas' independence, Bowen began to contemplate spiritual realities and saw himself clearly as a *"wicked young man."* He loved the honor and glory of being recognized as a valiant soldier, but the desire to give his life to Christ was stronger. He resigned his commission and returned to Georgia, saying, *"What profit would it be to my soul in eternity even if I had risen to be the greatest general of the age? The glory of this world passeth away, but the love of God — our love of God — abideth forever."*

When Bowen became a Christian in October of 1840, he exclaimed, *"I obtained hope in Christ and was soon after baptized in the name of the adorable Trinity. My happiness in those days was more than language can express."* He immediately felt a desire to speak to others about Christ. Over the course of the next several years, he grew in grace as he preached in numerous churches throughout the state of Georgia. A voracious reader, Bowen also grew in knowledge. After reading British missionary reports from Africa, he began to develop an interest in taking the Gospel to the interior of that continent.

Very few Christians were willing to consider such a hazardous undertaking, but God had uniquely shaped Thomas Jefferson Bowen for this mission. He wrote the Foreign Mission Board (SBC) and asked them to consider opening a work in *"Central Africa."* He said, *"If I should only live long enough to plant the Redeemer's standard on those bulwarks of heathenism as an ensign for others I trust my labor would not be in vain."* He received a favorable response from the Board and was soon appointed as a Southern Baptist missionary to Africa. The Board insisted that he not go alone; they asked for volunteers to join him. A new missionary appointee, Henry Goodale, who had been headed to China, changed his plans and teamed up with Bowen. Bowen and Goodale sailed for Africa from Providence, Rhode Island, in December of 1849.

They were filled with joy when they landed in Monrovia, the capital of the newly independent nation of Liberia, on February 8, 1850. Liberia was a country that had been established by freed slaves from the United States. Bowen, with his keen powers of observation, said, *"Our first employment ashore was to look at everything within our reach, and to inquire into everything we could think of."*

Bowen was pleased that many of the inhabitants of Liberia were Christians, but he lamented how few had a heart for reaching the lost of the continent. However, his sights were set on reaching native Africans farther up the "Slave Coast" and into the interior. He and his faithful missionary companion set off to explore and to evangelize inland. Goodale became ill, declining for a month before he finally died. Bowen was overcome with grief. He wrote, *"There are not many who can appreciate the sorrow and loneliness of a man who buries his beloved and only companion in the wilds of Africa."*

Refusing to quit, Bowen returned to the coast and sailed to Badagry, a port city on the edge of what is now known as Nigeria. This was the beginning of one of the greatest missionary endeavors in Southern Baptist history. Bowen opened the door; many would follow him over the next one hundred and fifty years.

Bowen traveled inland to the city of Abeokuta, which had an estimated 60,000 inhabitants. Abeokuta became his home for the next eighteen months. He set about learning the Yoruba language and culture, meticulously recording every grammatical principle of the language in his notebook. Bowen's commitment to language acquisition set a high standard for future cross-cultural missionaries. He said, *"The one great fault of some missionaries is a desire to discharge their duties with the least possible trouble. They cannot endure the annoyance of intercourse with the natives; they cannot submit to the toil of mastering a barbarous tongue; they cannot preach and talk everywhere in addition to the chapel services."*

The city of Abeokuta was the headquarters of the anti-slavery forces. The coastal cities had all fallen under the control of the pro-slavery Dahomey people. In surely one of the greatest ironies in the history of Southern Baptist missions, Thomas Jefferson Bowen stood with the anti-slavery forces in their battle against the attacking pro-slavery forces of King Gezo. Missionary Bowen, ever the soldier, stood on the city wall shouting encouragements and instructions to the Abeokuta warriors during the fight. He exhorted them *"to stand firm, to hold their fire, and to take good aim."*

The attacking forces were over 16,000 strong (10,000 men and 6,000 fierce women, known as Amazons). The battle was vicious and bloody, but at the end of the day, the anti-slavery forces of Abeokuta repelled their attackers. Bowen's part was small and seemingly insignificant, but when compared to the British missionaries, who were safely tucked away miles from the city, Bowen was remarkable. His stand with the citizens of Abeokuta opened the door of invitation to other cities in the region.

Bowen was progressing in his labors, but his being alone took a terrible toll on him. He lamented in a letter sent home:

> *I beg to be remembered in the fervent, effectual prayers of the brethren. Besides all of my other troubles, I have many painful conflicts with the flesh and the devil... I had counted the costs for months in the midst of conflicts between selfishness and duty. I had become willing to live a life of suffering and die among heathens, without one kind hand to wipe away the death sweat from my brow... But bodily afflictions are small compared with what*

> *I have suffered on account of my exile from home,*
> *and friends, and Christian privileges. For me, there*
> *is no sympathizing friend, with whom I can take*
> *sweet counsel; no kindred spirit with whom I can*
> *write in supplications and praise.*

At the point of his greatest distress—almost two years after leaving America—Bowen received his first letters from home. These letters, along with his first paycheck, buoyed his spirit and enabled him to make a long trek to the interior. On this journey, he was shut out of some towns but welcomed in others. One town that welcomed him was Bi-Olorun-Pelu, and he preached there for several days to large crowds.

Among the hearers was a middle-aged woman, named Oyindola, who came back day after day to listen. One morning, Oyindola presented herself to Bowen with a beaming face and declared that she had trusted Christ as her Savior. The next day she returned with her idols, which she gave up, and requested baptism. She was the first person converted through Bowen's ministry. He decided not to baptize her because he was dubious about leaving a lone convert in that city, and he was itching to travel farther inland. He later regretted his poor decision.

Among Southern Baptists, Bowen's work was stirring great interest and respect. In 1853, the Board glowingly reported in its minutes, *"Solitary, but with the companionship of God's Spirit; helpless, but with the strength of Jesus; our missionary has penetrated unknown regions, traversed mountains and plains untrodden before by white man's feet, and preached in the middle of the Dark Continent the Gospel of Jesus, till then unheard."*

Bowen pressed on to the city of Ijaiye, whose leader, King Kumi, welcomed him with open arms. Bowen thoroughly scouted the city and decided it would be his future base of operations. Exhausted and with no funds to build a mission house, he returned overland to Abeokuta. He decided his best course of action would be to go back to America for reinforcements. After an arduous sea journey, he arrived in America and set off on a whirlwind tour to raise awareness and support for the African mission.

After six months in America, he returned to Africa with five new recruits. One of them, Lurenna Davis, had become his wife on May 31, 1853. She was burning with missionary zeal and was firmly committed to reaching Africans with the good news of salvation. Lurenna proved to be Bowen's greatest human blessing and his loyal companion through the dark waters that lay ahead. Bowen, amazed by her fortitude, said, *"She never faltered at any difficulty, or uttered a word of complaint against any of the troubles we encountered."*

The next three years are described as "the most heroic and tragic" in the history of the Baptist mission to Nigeria. The day after their arrival in 1853, Lurenna's diary records a truth that would overwhelmingly mark this period, *"August 30—Sickness."* More often than not, the missionaries were sick, terribly sick. One of the couples, the Dennards, died; the other missionaries (the Lacys) were so sick they were forced to return to America.

The Bowens had one great joy during these first months in Africa; a healthy baby daughter, Mary Yoruba Bowen, was born on February 25, 1854. She was the first Southern Baptist MK born in Yoruba. Sadly, she fell ill, and just three months later, she died. Lurenna wrote in her diary, *"May 28, 1854—This morning about*

9 o'clock the spirit of our only earthly treasure took its flight to the heavenly worlds. Our dear child is dead! We buried her body this evening at 5 o'clock. Stillness and loneliness fill the house, we are <u>very</u>, <u>very</u> sad, but our hope is in the Lord 'for he is good, his mercy endureth forever.'"

Not long after their baby's death, the Bowens proceeded all alone to their original destination: the interior city of Ijaiye. The work progressed well; Bowen built a little mud and thatch chapel where he preached daily to the throngs who came to hear. A man and a woman professed faith and were baptized. Later that year, when a new FMB missionary arrived, they baptized three more converts.

The year 1855 was noted for the construction of a mission house that would also serve as an infirmary for sick missionaries. During that year, Bowen intensified his Gospel ministry and reported, *"Our preaching labors are incessant and ardent, every corner of Ijaiye heard the Gospel."* Most notably, the year marked the opening of Baptist work in Ogbomosho, which became the vital center of the work. Additionally, Bowen preached in the Muslim city of Ilorin. It is highly probable that Bowen was the first Southern Baptist missionary to preach in a Muslim city. Initially, it seemed as if the king of Ilorin would welcome Bowen to establish a mission there, but the king changed his mind. The Bowens' health continued to deteriorate. It became apparent in 1856 that they needed to journey to America where they could recuperate. Little did they know, they would never return to Africa.

Despite very poor health, Bowen threw himself into the task of preparing his manuscript about Africa. The following year (1857) his book *Central Africa: Adventures and Missionary Labors* was published. The book was filled with valuable information and observations: part travelogue, part ethnography, part history of Africa, and part history of missions in Africa. Additionally, it presented a vision for future missionary strategies. It remains a valuable source for the study of African culture and history and manifests the profound insight and intelligence of T. J. Bowen.

The Smithsonian Institute published Bowen's second book *Grammar and Dictionary of the Yoruba People*. This unique contribution was highly regarded for its scholarship and served as a standard text on the Yoruban language for decades.

With these projects completed, Bowen longed to return to Africa. However, the Board realized that his health was too poor for such an undertaking and declined to send him back to the continent that was fast becoming known as "the white man's graveyard." A few months later, they did accept Bowen's offer to become the first FMB missionary to Brazil. Thomas, Lurenna, and a new baby girl Lulu arrived in Brazil in April of 1859. They resided there for a little less than two years. Bowen's health worsened, and he was greatly discouraged by the intense hostility of the Brazilians to the preaching of the Gospel. The cost of living in Rio was vastly higher than it had been in Africa, and Bowen was severely underfunded for such a venture.

Bowen was encouraged for a short time when he met and conversed with slaves from Yoruba. The slaves were astonished to hear a white man speaking their language. Bowen thought he might have found a new place of ministry among the Yoruban diaspora. These hopes were short-lived because his meetings with slaves were reported to the Brazilian officials, who feared he was preaching a message of rebellion. Worst of all, Bowen's physical pains increased dramatically and led to a mental breakdown.

He became so incapacitated that Lurenna made the decision for the family to return to the USA. She wrote to the Corresponding Secretary of the Board, *"It is with much sorrow that I hasten to inform you that we are compelled to leave our field of labor in this country and return home."* She revealed that her husband's condition was worse than anyone had imagined, and if they remained in Brazil, *"he would certainly lose his reason and die away soon."*

Bowen was devastated that his missionary career had come to an end, but his physical and mental health had failed so badly that all hope of continuing had to be abandoned. They lived with Lurenna's parents in Greensboro, Georgia, which only added to Bowen's humiliation. The Civil War broke out just as they arrived, and Bowen enlisted to serve as a chaplain, but there is no record that he actually served.

The last fourteen years of Bowen's life are deeply sad and painful. Biographers of Bowen have struggled with what to say. Many have chosen to pull a veil of privacy over his afflictions. They fear the truth will tarnish Bowen's accomplishments, but we do no favors to the cause of Christ when we paint missions and missionaries only with bright colors. Bright colors are never the entire story for any of us in this fallen world of dark lines and shadows.

Bowen had suffered from malaria, yellow fever, and severe dysentery for years. In his efforts to alleviate the pain, he began taking laudanum, a derivative of opium. One of Bowen's biographers says, "Laudanum was routinely prescribed at the time to treat pain, diarrhea and dysentery. Although widely used to allay pain and of significant value to the medical profession, it was known that opium was addictive. Tolerance, along with physical dependence, often developed so that the dose had to be increased to obtain pain relief." By that time, it was well attested that prolonged use of the drug led to mental deterioration and hallucinations. Both were obvious in Bowen.

His restlessness increased, and he would slip away from home for months on end. Like a vagabond, he rode the rails back and forth to Texas and Florida, working odd jobs along the way. He referred to this period as his *"wandering years."* He also resorted to the use of alcohol to make it through the nightmare he was living. He recognized how desperate his situation was and voluntarily checked himself into a mental hospital, where he lived—on and off—for the remainder of his life.

Lurenna wrote Secretary Taylor and explained the tragic history of her husband's illness and addictions:

> *It is nearly six weeks since my dear husband went to the Asylum. He was perfectly conscious of his condition and deplored it as much as any of us. He would often say "Unless there is something done for me, I shall be totally ruined." His mind, which has been affected since '58, became more disordered during our stay in S.A., and since our return to this country (which I hoped would restore him) his lucid intervals have grown shorter and less frequent until it became seldom that he was himself. His physical suffering being very great, he resorted to stimulants to allay them. As a natural consequence as his thirst for those stimulants increased, he would lose his self control and give himself up to the use of them, for a week or longer at a time. He*

*had strange hallucinations such as hearing unreal
sounds, seeing and talking with persons who have
been dead many years. Sometimes he did not rec-
ognize me as his wife, and had an increasing dis-
position to get away from my influence. He also
had an inclination to stroll off from home, particu-
larly at night.*

Bowen turned sixty in 1874, and near the end of that year, he checked himself into the asylum one last time. He died at the mental hospital in Milledgeville, Georgia, on November 25, 1875. He was buried in an unmarked grave. One month prior to his death, he wrote his final letter to Lurenna, instructing her to say little about him upon his death. He was profoundly ashamed of the man he had become. He wrote, *"To say much about me in my present state, alone, broken-hearted, diseased and in want, would be worse than cruel mockery."* Most of his Christian brothers and sisters had turned their backs on him. They only saw the sin into which he had fallen.

Bowen felt the sting of his sin and of his addiction. A few years before his death, he wrote a poem to the church in Greensboro, Georgia, where Lurenna continued to live, asking for their forgiveness. He said:

*Dear Brethren, unto you and God
My sins and follies I confess;
Dark are the paths which I have trod
And full of pain and wretchedness*

Full well I know I never can
Climb to the point where once I stood
I ask it not of God or man;
My sole desire is to be good

And being good to be once more
A useful servant of my race;
Not useful, as I was before,
But as an evidence of grace

How should we remember Thomas Jefferson Bowen? As a heroic missionary pioneer marked by bold faith—YES! As a frail, flawed and sinful saint—yes. Above all, he wanted to be remembered *"as an evidence of grace."* If that alone is true of any of us, nothing greater can be said. Even so, Bowen is not forgotten everywhere. In South Georgia, there is an association of Baptist churches—where he often ministered—named in Bowen's honor. In Nigeria the Baptists have flourished, and they have not forgotten the man who opened the door and blazed the trail for them to hear the Gospel. Bowen University, a ministry of Nigerian Baptists, is named in his honor, as is the Bowen University Teaching Hospital. He would be astounded that his name is a sweet aroma across that land. But I imagine nothing was more astounding to Bowen than Jesus' welcoming him into His presence as **an evidence of His grace**. The day is coming when our struggle with sin, disease, and decay will be over. We will be at Jesus' feet singing, *"ransomed, healed, restored, forgiven, Evermore His praises sing. Alleluia! Alleluia! Praise the everlasting King!"*

Bowen's life is an instructive blessing for us all. Thank God for our bold missionary brothers and sisters! Pray for them with greater urgency, fervor, sympathy, and compassion. We are engaged in a fight against Satan and the powers of darkness, and our missionaries are on the frontlines. Cover them with prayer. Treat them with mercy and compassion when they struggle and fall. They are still warriors for Christ, even when they are wounded.

T.A. and Mary Reid, missionaries to Nigeria

Chapter Eight

MARY REID

d.o.b. unknown-1858
"Though He Slay Me, Yet Will I Trust Him"
Job 13:15a

F ollowing God's call to missionary service is a great joy and
blessing. However, many parents struggle with releasing their
children to pursue the missionary call. The story of Mary Canfield
Reid illustrates this conflict.

The date of Mary Canfield's birth in South Carolina is unknown
to us. While Mary was growing up, she occasionally attended a
Roman Catholic Church but did not have a personal faith. She
was soundly converted to Jesus Christ at the First Baptist Church
of Washington, Georgia, under the ministry of Pastor H. A. Tupper.

Not long after her conversion, Mary told Pastor Tupper she
sensed that God was calling her to Africa as a missionary. Her
interest was so evident and intense that Corresponding Secretary
James B. Taylor paid her a visit. Despite her heart for the work,
Secretary Taylor informed her that the board would not send her
out as a single woman missionary. Mary was not deterred. She
wrote her pastor a letter, expressing that her meeting with James

Taylor had not changed her mind in the least. She was *bound* to this calling by God.

In God's providence, T. A. Reid (a young Georgia man) was sensing God's call on his life to be a missionary to Africa about the same time. Reid's father was a bi-vocational Baptist preacher with a large family. His father received little or no salary from the church, so T. A. had limited educational opportunities in his early years. Doors began to open, culminating with the opportunity to study at Mercer University. As a student at Mercer, he was mentored and assisted greatly by P. H. Mell and John L. Dagg. In September of 1856, the Rehoboth Association of Georgia elected him as their missionary to Africa.

When a meeting was arranged, T. A. came to visit Mary in Washington, Georgia, in May of 1857. They liked each other; a strong attachment quickly developed between them. There was, however, a serious roadblock in the path of their relationship and missionary plans. Mary's mother, Mrs. Haines, was not a Christian and adamantly opposed her daughter's missionary call. Mary invited Pastor Tupper for a conversation with her mother about that topic. The following dialogue took place between them:

Mrs. Haines: "So, sir, you wish to take Mary from me, and send her to Africa to die?"

Pastor Tupper: "It is a fearful thought, madam, that the separation between you and your daughter may be an eternal one."

Mrs. Haines: "What do you mean, sir?"

Pastor Tupper: "The Bible says there shall be an impassable gulf between those who love and obey God and those who do not."

Mrs. Haines: "Do you, sir, say that Mary and I must be separated? That she shall go to Africa?"

Pastor Tupper: "No, madam; but I say that she will be saved; and you must be lost if you continue in your sins. Will you allow us to engage in prayer that you and Mary may be united forever?"

The next day Pastor Tupper called again, and yet again the next day, but Mary's mother seemed uninterested in her own spiritual condition. The following day Pastor Tupper returned to find Mrs. Haines under deep conviction of sin.

Toward the end of their conversation, she exclaimed, "If the Lord will only forgive my iniquity!"

Pastor Tupper replied, "Would you let Mary go to Africa?"

Mary's mother stood up from her chair and emphatically proclaimed, "It would be the greatest honor of my life!"

The Holy Spirit had changed her heart. Everyone in the room burst into praise and thanksgiving to God. Mrs. Haines had trusted Jesus as her Savior from sin! Immediately, her heart was opened for her daughter to go to Africa to tell others of the same salvation she had just experienced.

The following Sunday morning, Pastor Tupper baptized Mrs. Haines. Two days later, Mary Canfield and T. A. Reid were married on May 26, 1857. They were immediately set apart by the First Baptist Church of Washington, Georgia, as their missionaries to Africa. The congregation lavished them with love and support during the hectic days that followed. They left Georgia two months later and traveled to New York. From there they sailed for Africa on August 7, 1857, arriving at their field of service six weeks later.

Mary wrote a letter to the Board from the city of Lagos. She was happy to be in Africa but was struggling with a sense of homesickness. She said, *"I must confess my heart saddens and the strong flood of feelings overflows its banks. But why grow sad? We walk by faith, not by sight; and walking thus, faith points, with holy hand, towards Heaven, re-assuring us that 'He who sent thee has promised to sustain thee.'"* She also recounts the tender story of her husband's returning to the schooner (*The Hanover*) with a gift for her—a flower from the shore. Although it was a simple four o'clock flower that had withered, it meant much to her because it was the first flower she had from the soil of Africa.

Seven months later, a simple, hand-hewn coffin was lowered into that same African soil in the town of Ogbomosho. It was Mary's coffin, made by her grieving husband. She had been well— even vibrant—until a few days before her death. The "African fever," as it was called, seized her as it did countless other missionaries, and her life ebbed away. She died on May 17, 1858. Her death was just a few days shy of her first wedding anniversary. In her last recorded words, she quoted from the book of Job, *"**Though He slay me, yet will I trust Him**."*

Her husband was in a state of shock, but he faithfully continued to serve as a single missionary in Africa. T. A. Reid suffered terrible hardships and extreme isolation. He was cut off from the outside world during a long period of inter-tribal warfare. No one heard from him for more than two years. He later wrote:

> *I was very loth to leave my post till the war was over, but necessity seemed to demand it. I was destitute of almost everything. My clothing was worn out, and no food but native, and that not good, because of the scarcity of cowries to buy food with. Many times, for several days, I have lived on one cent's worth of food per day. Sometimes, for five or ten days, I*

*did not taste meat of any kind. I was twenty-seven
months without seeing the face of a white person.*

His health was broken, necessitating his return to America in 1864. He wanted to go back to Yoruba with several black Christian families by his side to strengthen the work. Reid also sought to publish a book about his experiences in Africa. Both plans failed. In time he re-married and pastored several congregations in South Carolina, Arkansas, and Kentucky.

The First Baptist Church of Washington, Georgia, was profoundly affected by the devoted service of Mary and T. A. Reid. Their pastor, Henry Allen Tupper, left them in 1873 to become the second Corresponding Secretary of the Foreign Mission Board (SBC). Tupper was a great missions leader for Southern Baptists and a resolute supporter of women missionaries, married *and* single. One of the first single women missionaries sent out during his tenure was Lottie Moon.

Mary's church sent a tombstone to mark her grave in Africa. A later missionary, who stumbled across that grave in the corner of the mission premises, prayed that Mary's work would remain. He said, *"I hoped that when death calls for me, I too might be found pointing the same people to the same Saviour. The silent voice from that grave has inspired me with greater desire and determination to labor while it is day, for the night cometh."*

Mary's mother was heartbroken upon hearing of her daughter's death, and her own death was not far behind. However, death did not separate them but *re-united* them forever in God's presence. The LORD had used Mary's call to leave her mother and go to Africa in order to call Mrs. Haines—late in life—to Himself. God works in mysterious ways; do not despise His eternal Kingdom. It is a land without shadows, without night, without death, and without goodbyes.

MATTHEW T. YATES
MISSIONARY TO CHINA
1846-1888

Matthew Yates, missionary to Shanghai

Chapter Nine

MATTHEW YATES

1819-1888
Towering Pioneer of Southern Baptist Missions

"But grow in the grace and knowledge of our Lord
and Savior Jesus Christ. To him be the glory both
now and to the day of eternity. Amen." **2 Peter 3:18**

M atthew Tyson Yates continued to grow. His continued
growth set him apart as a remarkable man and missionary.
Between the ages of twenty-eight and fifty, he grew two inches in
height, reaching 6 feet 2½ inches. His full fighting weight was 244
pounds. He was a towering physical presence in Shanghai, China,
where he served as a missionary for over forty years. Yet, his physical size and growth were incidental to the true size and growth of
Yates. He was a *spiritual giant*, who continued throughout his life
to grow in the grace and knowledge of our Lord and Savior, Jesus
Christ. He was a towering pioneer of Southern Baptist Missions,
whose example has the power to inspire the next generation of
missionaries. He was the best-known and most respected Southern
Baptist missionary of the nineteenth century. Yates went to China
when Lottie Moon was six years old.

Matthew was born to William and Delilah Yates in Wake County, North Carolina, on January 8, 1819. He was the second of ten children, and his father was a hard-working farmer and a leader in their local congregation, Mount Pisgah Baptist Church. When the church hosted itinerant country preachers, they stayed with the Yates family. One of these preachers, whom they affectionately called "Father Purefoy," had a profound impact on young Matthew. Matthew said, regrettably, most adults never spoke to children about spiritual things, but Rev. John Purefoy was different. One day as he was leaving the Yates' home, he asked Matthew *if* he prayed.

Matthew said, *"No,"* because he didn't know *what* to pray.

Father Purefoy instructed him to pray, "Lord, be merciful to me a sinner." When he returned for his next visit, he asked Matthew, "Have you been praying?"

Matthew said, *"No, I don't know where to pray."* Preacher Purefoy instructed him to find a private place in the woods that he could designate as his special spot for prayer.

A terrifying experience in a thunderstorm motivated Matthew to find the suggested place of prayer. As he prayed, he began to understand that in God's eyes he was a sinner, who desperately needed mercy and grace. After a long struggle, he was converted. Rev. Purefoy's interest in the spiritual condition of a young person impressed itself deeply upon him. Matthew gained and grew in a commitment to the spiritual conversion and discipleship of children. He urged Christian adults to speak to children—early and often—about spiritual matters, especially their souls. Matthew taught that children needed to be blessed, encouraged, and given opportunities to serve. Matthew had learned to pray as a child, and from then on, prayer was at the center of his life.

Immediately after Matthew's conversion, a new prayer entered his heart, *"Lord, what wilt thou have me do?"* New life in Christ naturally translates into a deep desire to serve Him. One Sunday afternoon, Matthew was enabled to make a complete surrender of his life to God. On his knees he prayed, *"Here, Lord, I give myself to thee, use me for thy glory whensoever and wheresoever it seemeth good in thy sight."* The foundation was laid. Matthew was truly converted and consecrated to Christ.

He still did not know how God would use him, but he wanted to prepare to preach the Gospel of Jesus Christ. About that time a blessed providence happened in his life. He read a missionary biography! Reflecting on that event, he wrote, *"My attention was first directed to the condition of the heathen world from reading the memoirs of Mrs. Judson, soon after obtaining, I trust, the remission of my sins. Frequently did I weep for hours, while following my plow or using my trowel, when I would reflect that the poor heathen, who knew nothing of Jesus Christ, the only Saviour of the world, must die and appear before God to be judged according to their works in this world."* This not only turned Matthew's heart toward reaching the unreached, but also it taught him the importance of hearing direct reports and stories from missionaries in order to cultivate an evangelistic spirit.

Matthew continued to grow in this area throughout his life. The address he made during his commissioning service was on the importance of "missionary intelligence." His point was to show the importance of knowledge about missions and missionaries to the growth of missionary spirit and support among the churches. He practiced what he preached. Throughout all of his life, Matthew wrote countless letters back to the USA to fan the flame for taking the Gospel to the ends of the earth. Two full-length biographies and numerous articles later written about Yates solidified Southern Baptists as a missionary people.

Matthew Yates would not agree with those people who think that being *called* to missionary service means one is automatically *equipped* for missionary service. Yates felt he lacked the necessary education to carry out an effective ministry for Christ, so he went back to school. After much effort, he finished high school at the age of twenty-one, but his education was not over. He was introduced to Samuel Wait, the president of Wake Forest College, who personally invited him to attend that school. Yates protested that he was too old and lacked the funds for such an undertaking. Wait replied, "Never mind, never mind, where there is a will there is a way. The State Convention will help you; come to college, come next session."

Matthew Yates became the first recipient of a ministerial scholarship from the Baptist State Convention of North Carolina. College was a long, hard struggle, but Yates completed his degree five years later in 1846. He was not a brilliant student, but he was a hardworking student, and his perseverance would bear much fruit. He maintained a life-long affection for Wake Forest College and appreciated the preparation for ministry he received.

The Foreign Mission Board appointed Yates as a missionary to China after his graduation in 1846. In the fall of that same year, he married Eliza Mooring. They became a remarkable team, and it was later said of them, "Adam and Eve made one man. These two people improved on that; they made one missionary. There is nothing that Yates ever did in China that could have been so well done without Mrs. Yates."

When the Southern Baptist Convention was formed in 1845, Baptists from America had already been engaged in missionary work in South China for a decade. The transfer of missionary J. Lewis Shuck to the FMB led Southern Baptists to continue the work that was already in place. However, the FMB also desired to open their first entirely new field of service. They set their sights on Shanghai, China. Arriving on September 13, 1847, Matthew and Eliza Yates were the first Southern Baptist missionaries in that city. Shanghai was their home for more than forty years.

One of Yates' influential contributions to Southern Baptist missions was his emphasis on language acquisition. Many missionaries of the time were content to speak through interpreters. They were not willing to engage in the years of hard work it takes to become proficient in a foreign language. Yates realized *then* what we often take for granted *now*; **being able to speak to people directly in their heart language is vital to missionary effectiveness**.

Yates' early progress in learning the Shanghai dialect of Chinese was threatened when he suddenly developed serious problems with his eyes. The standard process for language learning was to study the written Chinese classics with a bilingual teacher. This was intended to enable the missionary to read and write a formal version of the complex Chinese language. Yates was forced to abandon that method of learning, so he devoted himself to acquiring the spoken language of the ordinary people on the street. Yates explained, *"In pursuance of this object, much time was spent among the people in the tea shops, listening to them as they talked, and asking and answering questions. In this way I learned the spoken language, in a great measure by ear."* His sight was gradually restored, but he continued with his new method of language acquisition.

Yates had a keen musical ear. He learned the language so well it was said that if a Chinese person shut his eyes, he could not distinguish between Yates' speaking of Chinese and that of a native. However, with the help of a scribe, Yates also made many literary contributions. He developed a Chinese/English dictionary and wrote *First Lessons in Chinese*, which aided subsequent missionaries to learn the language much more quickly. He wrote tracts in Chinese and translated others from English. However, his crowning achievement was the translation of all the books of the New Testament (except Revelation) into the Shanghai dialect of Chinese. The first thousand copies of his Chinese New Testament were delivered on the same day his body was laid to rest in the foreign cemetery in Shanghai in 1888.

Yates had one desire above all others for learning to speak Chinese—to preach Christ to sinners. For decades he did this almost daily, while insisting, *"Our great work in preaching is to present the love of God in Christ Jesus as the only antidote for all the fears and woes of this people...The blessing of the Holy Spirit upon the pure Gospel, faithfully preached and circulated, is the only power that can enlighten the minds of the Chinese."*

The response was slow in the early years but began to increase as time passed. To the very end, Yates never wavered in his confidence in the importance of preaching. He declared, *"What we need to insure permanent success is to have constantly on the field a good corps of devoted and effective preachers. The longer I remain in the field, the more thoroughly I am convinced that preaching is the great lever by which this vast empire is to be raised from the abyss of darkness"* Yates did not aim for impressive numbers of church members but for genuine conversions. He said, *"We aim at solid work, no clap-trap, no sensational enterprises to write about. We believe thoroughly in schools; but for evangelizing agency, our reliance is on the law and the gospel. The Lord bless his own appointed way."* Yates was thoroughly committed to planting and developing strong, biblical churches. Matthew and Eliza carefully instructed every new believer, and they practiced formative and corrective discipline in the church. They taught the following four principles to the members:

- *The church is made up of a converted and evangelical membership; to admit persons for any other reasons will paralyze the whole church.*
- *Christians are disciples of Christ, not disciples of the missionary.*
- *Christians, as disciples of Christ, should become thoroughly acquainted with His teachings. They should commit to memory precious and practical portions of the Bible.*
- *Christians are individually responsible to God, and each member is called to make efforts to show and spread the faith to their family and community.*

Another contribution that Yates made to Southern Baptist missions was his relentless effort to call for new missionary recruits. Yates' first biographer, Charles E. Taylor, was deeply moved as he read the appeals that Yates made—year after year—for more missionaries. Sadly, those appeals often fell on closed ears and hard hearts back in America. In one of his typical pleas, Yates wrote from Shanghai in 1850, *"Are there not young men in the Southern churches whose hearts glow with love to the Saviour and melt with compassion for the heathen? I would ask them upon what grounds they have decided that it is not their duty to consecrate themselves to this work. And I would beseech them to be certain that the arguments with which they have been hushing the voice of conscience will stand the test of the final judgment."*

Matthew and Eliza served alone for more than twenty years. Sickness, death, re-location, and lack of reinforcements within the Shanghai missionary team led to this deplorable situation. Taylor, the biographer, cried out in response to Yates' unheeded petitions, "Oh, Christ, forgive us that we let thy servant—and ours—struggle so many years alone and single handed against the overwhelming odds."

Yates had a deep and abiding trust in God's plan and power to reach all the peoples of the earth with the Gospel. Nevertheless, he realized that God had ordained to accomplish His mission through human instruments. As Yates was dying in 1888, a young missionary recruit, R. T. Bryan, cared for him. Bryan records the following, *"One day, while rubbing his foot, I looked up and saw tears running down his cheeks, then he sobbed a few times. I wiped away the tears."*

And Yates said, *"So much work, and I can't do any of it."*

Bryan answered, *"God can have it done, Father Yates."*

Yates replied, *"But God needs men."*

Yates felt deeply the need for a vast army of men and women missionaries to spread the Gospel to the ends of the earth. However, he did not think everyone should be a missionary. He said, *"As much as we need men, it will never do to appoint every man and woman who applies. From cranks, short horns, and men lacking common sense, good Lord deliver us!"*

On March 17, 1888, Yates' family and missionary co-laborers surrounded him as he lay sleeping in his bed. He stirred, rose up slightly, pointed upward, and then fell back into the bed. In that moment, he passed into the presence of Christ. A telegram soon went around the world declaring, "Yates dead." Though his earthly labors ended that day, his life has continued to bear fruit.

Matthew Yates embodies the missionary spirit. His faithfulness, his generosity, his love for Christ, and his compassion for the lost continue to inspire. Charles Taylor said, "That Yates in China did more to build up the kingdom of Christ in America than Yates in America could have done, will hardly be doubted. And, though no man can tell what noble structures are to be built upon the solid foundations laid by him in China, it may be questioned whether the reflex influence of his work upon the churches at home was not equal to the direct influence of his work abroad." Matthew and Eliza blazed the trail and laid a good foundation for all future Southern Baptist missionaries. Their influence for Christ is beyond our ability to measure.

Matthew, Eliza, and Annie Yates

REV. MATTHEW TYSON YATES, D.D.,
When 61 years old, and when he had been 37 years a missionary in China. Height, 6 feet 2 inches; weight, 244 pounds.

Yates, towering pioneer

Landrum Holmes, missionary to Shandong Province, China

Chapter Ten

LANDRUM HOLMES

1836-1861
The First Southern Baptist Missionary Murdered

"They were stoned, they were sawn in two, they
were killed with the sword. They went about in
skins of sheep and goats, destitute, afflicted, mistreated — of whom the world was not worthy...."

Hebrews 11:37-38a

James Landrum Holmes was born on May 16, 1836, in Preston
County, which is now a part of West Virginia. He was raised,
confirmed, and converted to Christ as a Methodist. Shortly after his
profession of faith, Landrum felt called by God to go to China as
a missionary. While dating a Baptist girl (perhaps Sallie), he came
across an article by Rev. Richard Fuller, one of the most important
preachers and pastors in early Southern Baptist life.

Landrum was captivated by the article and wrote to the editor,
Franklin Wilson in Baltimore, who sent him a copy of Fuller's work
Baptism and the Terms of Communion. He read it eagerly and was
thoroughly convinced by Fuller's biblical arguments on the subject.
He promptly presented himself for baptism into the Cheat River

Baptist Church. He was one of thirteen people baptized by Pastor
D. B. Purington in the year 1855.

After his baptism, Landrum was on the move; Baltimore,
Maryland, became his home. He joined a new church plant,
Franklin Square Baptist, in the growing West End of the city. His
pastor was Rev. George Boardman Taylor, who later became a
pioneer Southern Baptist missionary in Italy. George was a son of
James Taylor, Corresponding Secretary (the first) of the Foreign
Mission Board in Richmond. Editor Franklin Wilson, to whom
Landrum had written about Fuller's article, was also a member of
the Franklin Square Church.

Wilson financially supported Landrum, enabling him to attend
and graduate from Columbian College in Washington, D.C.
Columbian was founded by Luther Rice in 1821. The connection
to Luther Rice meant that the school was profoundly "missionary"
in spirit. It was an ideal training ground for Landrum and many
other foreign missionaries.

Landrum already knew Sallie Little, the woman who would
become his wife. In fact, Sallie was living in Baltimore during this
time and was also a student. Landrum was ordained to the Gospel
ministry by the Franklin Square Church in June of 1858. Earlier
that year, Landrum had written a letter to Sallie's mother, asking
her blessing on their plans to wed. He wrote, *"I cannot offer your
daughter a brilliant worldly prospect; our life will, on the contrary,
probably be one of toil and trial. Looking upon the subject in a
mere worldly point of view, I might hesitate to ask one whom I hold
in so high esteem to share such a lot with me. But we propose to live
and labor and die in the work of spreading the Gospel of Christ."*

Sallie's mother was thrilled! Mrs. Little was a strong Christian and desired to be a foreign missionary herself but was unable to do so. In response to her daughter's commitment to be a missionary, Mrs. Little was "as happy as King David must have been when God permitted Solomon to build the Temple." Her support was vitally important to Sallie, not only then, but also in the difficult years ahead.

Landrum and Sallie sailed from New York to Shanghai in August of 1858 on the ship *Falcon* and arrived in February of 1859. In Shanghai they began to learn Chinese and to familiarize themselves with the culture and climate. Landrum was remarkable in many ways and learned Chinese very quickly. A missionary named Helen Nevius later wrote of Holmes, "He was a person whose peculiar loveliness of character made him a favorite with every one. Handsome, talented, ardent, with very winning manners, he was peculiarly fitted for usefulness among the Chinese, to whom such qualities are very attractive."

Only one year after his arrival, Landrum was invited by the US Consul to accompany him to Peking as an interpreter. Landrum also visited Nanking and met with various leaders of the Taiping Rebellion, exploring mission opportunities in areas under their control. He was not favorably impressed, but he did achieve an open door of civility with them.

Landrum was not satisfied that Shanghai ought to be his field of labor. He continued to explore opportunities for a new mission station farther north. The province of Shandong was on the verge of being opened to foreigners, and Landrum was drawn to work in that region. He liked many things about that "pioneer" area, including the cooler climate.

Shandong was highly populated but had no major city like Shanghai. It is the birthplace of Confucius and home of Mount Tai, one of Daoism's Five Sacred Mountains. The famous Yellow River that runs through this province makes it an important agricultural area, but it is also prone to devastating floods and subsequent famines.

Landrum and Sallie visited the area in May of 1859 but were forced to return to Shanghai. When Landrum visited again, he lived for a period of time on a Chinese junk (boat) in the harbor. Every day he rowed to the city, preached the Gospel, and returned to the boat at night. He was privileged to be the first person to bring the Gospel of Jesus Christ to that province. Because he desired to do more, he hoped the French Navy would open the city to foreigners. Finally, a treaty between the French and Chinese was reached. Landrum wrote on February 8, 1861, *"China is open to the preaching of the gospel in all its length and breadth."*

A great price was yet to be paid in order to get the Gospel into China, but the door was finally, fully open. Landrum and Sallie walked through that open door into the province of Shandong— blazing the trail for many other missionaries to follow. This would be the land of Lottie Moon, and in the 1930s, the great Shantung Revival!

Landrum's brother, Matthew Holmes, accompanied them to Shandong in order to open an import/export business. This business proved vital because the outbreak of the Civil War made it impossible for funds to reach them from Richmond. Landrum briefly worked with Matthew to provide for his family, but he saw every business contact as a precious opportunity to share the Gospel. Landrum's family was growing with the birth of their daughter,

Annie Kennedy Holmes. Blue-eyed, curly headed, and bubbly, little Annie brightened the home immensely. Things were looking up. In June of 1860, Landrum baptized the first convert in Shandong, a Chinese man named Chu San.

Despite their bright hopes for the future, warning clouds darkened the Shandong skies in 1861. The Taiping Rebellion, which had been raging in many areas of China since 1850, began to influence this northern province. The leadership of the Taipings was beginning to fall apart. Soldiers, who had fought in the rebellion, turned into bands of robbers, pillaging the countryside. One account of their atrocities reads:

> In 1861 Shantung experienced the terrible ravages of these "long-haired" rebels, really robber bands, allied in name only with Taiping Wang then ruling in Nanking. All loyal subjects of the Manchus wore the queue and shaved the head for an inch around the scalp. The rebels cut their queues, but were called "longhaired" because of the disordered locks hanging about their terrifying faces. In Central China the Taipings had shown some consideration for Christians. But not so in Shantung! They butchered old and young all along their path from West to East. Country people crowded into walled cities or made camps on steep hilltops, barricading themselves with stones. There they suffered torments from hunger and even more from thirst. In some places women and children were hidden in pits prepared for sweet potatoes. If a baby cried he

was speedily strangled lest he endanger the safety of all. Many women, who, because of bound feet, had no chance for escape, killed their children by hanging or drowning, then themselves. Wells were filled to the brim with their bodies.

While renegade soldiers ravaged the countryside, little Annie Holmes was seriously ill in Chefoo. Sallie wrote to Annie Kennedy, her best friend in America, on August 29, 1861, *"Oh Annie, our little Annie has gone home to heaven—her little body lies beside me now. She has gone to the "better land." The Lord gave, the Lord has taken away. Blessed be the name of the Lord. He is with me and sustains me now. She passed away yesterday at half past five. She was cutting her last teeth; they were all through, but her strength entirely failed. She passed away without a struggle."* In those years, foreigners were not allowed to be buried on the mainland. Little Annie's body was taken to a rocky island in the Chefoo harbor and buried there.

Six weeks after Annie's death, Landrum heard that a band of rebels was headed toward the coastal region where they lived. He ran to the nearby village of Chukee and warned the people to flee for their lives. Holmes and a Protestant Episcopal missionary, Thomas Parker, determined they would try to negotiate peace with the invaders. They hoped that Landrum's prior connection to the Taipings would deter the rebels' murderous march toward Chefoo. Holmes and Parker mounted their horses and boldly rode out to meet them. They did not return....

Matthew Holmes organized a search party that eventually found the bodies of the two missionaries. The search party met eyewitnesses who recounted that Holmes and Parker spent the night at an inn and left early the next morning to meet the rebels. One witness stated, "They dismounted from their horses before the rebels came up which I suppose was to disarm their enmity. A party of fifty or sixty rebels as soon as they saw them rushed upon them and surrounded them and without a word of parley immediately chopped them down."

The recovered bodies of the missionaries showed they had been horribly mutilated, and "Holmes had received ten wounds most of which were about the head inflicted with a sword or spear. All the upper portion of his person was burned. Apparently, he had fallen into a fire or upon a pile of fodder, which was afterward set on fire. Parker had some six or seven wounds most of which also were on his head. His right hand was cut through at the knuckle where the fingers join the hand." Landrum was twenty-five years old. He was the first, but sadly, not the last of our missionaries to be murdered. Sallie wrote the following poignant lines to her friend Annie on October 14, 1861, *"Oh Annie, Landrum is dead. Murdered by rebels. Pray for me."*

The rebels did reach the coast, but Landrum's warnings and the intervention of the French Navy saved those cities. More than seventy years later, the tiny village of Chukee still remembered Landrum Holmes' courageous efforts to save them. They ceremonially honored him twice a year and even erected a monument in his memory.

Landrum was dead, but the need to reach North China remained. Sallie did not leave her post but stayed despite her unbelievable losses. She wrote:

I could not leave the people Landrum has known and who have known him, while there is any hope of doing them good, and when they talk as they so often do that they are not afraid of me, my husband was a good man & gave his life for theirs, how willingly would I also give mine for them... life can never be the joy it once was to me, and to die and be with Landrum again would be joy, but I don't think I have just the right feeling about that. I know I think more of dying and being with Landrum than with my Saviour. Still I believe I am God's child and I don't think he will let me feel that way always, though through what other furnace of affliction I shall be called to pass before my heart is purified from its dross I do not know. He only in his infinite wisdom & love knows what is necessary... I know He will not forsake me. Not of me will it be said, joined to her idols let her alone. No, He will save me from my sins, save me from myself. But a life more precious than either of ours has been given for these heathen and I long to tell them of Him, but the way of doing this is very different than we often imagine.

We now turn to Sallie's story....

116

Landrum and Sallie Holmes wedding photo

Chapter Eleven

SALLIE HOLMES

1836-1914
Faithful Through Deep and Dark Waters

"When you pass through the waters, I will be with
you..."   **Isaiah 43:2**a

T wo weeks after the brutal murder of her husband, Sallie Holmes
wrote, "*I know, deep and dark as the waters are, my affliction
is nothing to compare with that of losing one so dear and yet having
no assurance of their eternal salvation... My consolation, my hope
rests in that Landrum trusted in Christ.*" Her confidence in Christ
and His Gospel enabled the widowed Sallie to remain in North
China as a tireless missionary worker over the next twenty years.

Not long before his own death, Landrum came home and told
Sallie that a fellow missionary had died. He was distraught and
said, "*If I thought I should die and leave you alone—leave you to
go all that long way back by yourself, I should find it hard to say,
'Thy will be done.'*"

Sallie replied, "*Landrum, I would not go back; I would stay
here and work.*" Sallie's strong and prophetic reply put Landrum
at ease and allowed him to continue his work.

Sallie struggled with profound grief for years. She wrote, *"I am miserable all the time and in agony often and this feeling is so overwhelming I am scarcely conscious of any other."* She found a beautiful poem by Landrum that comforted her deeply:

> *When thou art weeping o'er the wreck*
> *Of Hopes and joys long crushed*
> *I'll come and whisper in thine ear*
> *Of Joys that fade not,*
> *And hopes that will be realized*
> *In Heaven*

After reading Landrum's poem, Sallie was able to say, *"When I feel almost that I must die, so lonely, so dark is my life on Earth to be, my bright hopes so crushed, my deep joy, my happy, happy life all gone, I try to turn from these things, for I know he would point me to the joys that fade not and the hopes that will be realized in Heaven."*

Soon after Landrum's death, Sallie wrote to a friend in America, *"God has seen fit to give me the strongest earthly consolation that could be to one who has lost a husband of such a loving & lovely character. I expect to become again a mother of his dear child."* Landrum Jr. was born on June 29, 1862. Sallie moved to the nearby mission station at Tung Chau (Penglai) where she raised Landrum Jr. and engaged in many facets of missionary labor.

Sallie was born in Upperville, Virginia, on July 24, 1836. Her mother was a teacher, and her father was a dentist. She was well educated, and her love of learning translated into a desire to teach the children of China. During her missionary career, she started several schools and taught regularly for twenty years. Lottie Moon wrote, *"Mrs. Holmes has a girls' boarding school. The Chinese do not believe in educating women. Hence it is a very slow and difficult work to gather even a few girls for instruction. Very few of the women read at all. Mrs. Holmes' success has been gratifying... Her school is flourishing with every promise of increase & permanent success. She is a noble woman & an earnest worker."*

It is clear that Sallie's primary desire, as a teacher, was to introduce the children to God, Christ, the Gospel, and the Bible. She issued several Chinese editions of a religious training primer for young children: *The Peep of Day*. That sweet collection of Bible stories begins with a catechism:

My dear little Children—You have seen the sun in the sky.

Who put the sun in the sky? *God.*

Can you reach up so high? *No.*

Who holds up the sun, that it does not fall? *It is God.*

God lives in heaven; heaven is much higher than the sun.

Can you see God? *No.*

Yet he can see you, for God sees every thing.

Sallie longed for the conversion of her students to Christ, but she knew that the Holy Spirit had to change their hearts. She wrote:

I long for the conversion of these Chinese. I pray for it, but I do not know what is lacking in the spirit of my prayers. Something is lacking, I feel that, but whether it is something I am responsible for, or whether it is that God's time for an outpouring of

> *his Spirit has not come, and he withholds that spirit of prayer he sometimes gives his people, I do not know. Help me, Annie, if you can and offer up your prayers for the conversion of my scholars, and of the women who have heard from Mrs. Crawford and me the story, which should melt their hearts, but they are so hard and indifferent. Pray for the Holy Spirit's influence on these stony hearts.*

Sallie raised at least two Chinese boys in her home, along with Landrum Jr. Another female missionary who knew her well said Sallie was a very good and loving mother to all of those boys. It is hard to imagine how difficult her life must have been in those years—a widow, a mother, a teacher, and above all, a missionary.

Sallie enjoyed teaching, but her true love as a missionary was village-to-village evangelism. Along with her faithful missionary friend and co-laborer, Martha Crawford, she "sallied" out from Tung Chau to the surrounding villages to share the Gospel. Sallie was fearless. Martha was a bit more timid but no less committed. They recognized that in order for Chinese women to hear the Gospel, it would need to come from the lips of women. Chinese women were largely secluded in their homes and did not mix with men in public settings. Sallie said, *"Oh I so want to work while it is called today for the night cometh and it seems to me it is coming, rapidly. Oh help me by your prayers that I may tell these poor Chinese of a Saviour."*

Sallie and Martha would pack food, pick a direction, and set off to share the Gospel with the women of Shandong. Sometimes, they chose a village because it was the home of a girl in Sallie's boarding school in Tung Chau. Martha traveled in a *shentze*, which was a covered chair carried by several mules. Sallie found that she became dizzy and nauseous in the shentze, so she chose to ride a donkey. Sallie wrote, *"We generally go for three days of a week, and visit ten or twelve villages... I go on a donkey, slipping down easily to walk when I get tired of riding, and mounting again as easily when I am tired of walking."*

A missionary later said of them, *"Mrs. Holmes and Mrs. Crawford were tireless in visiting in the city and neighboring villages, giving the Good News in season and out of season. Mrs. Holmes went fearlessly forward entering doors where the invitation was only half-hearted or even wholly lacking."* The number of visits they made is astounding! Women in hundreds of villages and thousands of homes heard the Gospel because of Sallie's unstoppable desire for them to know the Savior.

Lottie Moon, who learned this kind of evangelism from Sallie and Martha, said, *"In city and in village, thousands of women will never hear the gospel until women bear it to them. They will admit women, but men cannot gain access to their homes, nor will they come to church. The only way for them to hear the good news of salvation is from the lips of foreign women. Are there not some, yea many, who find it in their hearts to say, "Here am I; send me"?* This situation remains true today. Christian women are still desperately needed to carry the Gospel to millions of women, who otherwise will not hear.

Sallie struggled with declining health and with an increasing desire to be reunited with Landrum Jr., who was attending college in Richmond, Virginia. Reluctantly, she left China, but China remained in her heart. Back in America she promoted missions, especially to

China, throughout the state of West Virginia where she lived the rest of her days.

Sallie had even more "deep and dark waters" through which to pass. Landrum Jr., who had become a medical doctor, is reported to have been an opium addict, who died of an overdose at the age of thirty. Of the two Chinese boys that Sallie raised, one initially professed faith in Christ but eventually turned his back on Christianity. The other boy, who had been rescued from starvation, became a successful businessman. He sent Sallie $600 every year—a very generous gift—to express his love and gratitude to her. Additionally, he endowed a school in her honor in the city of Tung Chau.

Sallie lived for the last twenty-two years of her life in Moundsville, West Virginia, on the banks of the Ohio River. At Sallie's death, the Moundsville paper wrote, "She has endured much trouble, more than falls to the lot of many people, but through it all she maintained that cheerful, hopeful spirit which characterized her as a true Christian." She was laid to rest beside her son in the Rose Hill Cemetery of Moundsville.

Nearly 7,000 miles away from that cemetery in Moundsville, lie the bodies of her husband and her daughter. They were buried side by side on an island in the harbor of Chefoo (Yentai). That island has been called by many names, including Lighthouse Island. No name could be more appropriate because it was through the Holmes family that the light of the Gospel first reached the Shandong province. Not long before her death in 1914, Sallie was shown photographs of a recently constructed church building in Chefoo, named Holmes Memorial Chapel. At the dedication, over 1,200 people packed into that building to worship Christ and to give thanks for His first ambassadors to Shandong—Landrum and Sallie Holmes. AMEN.

Chapter Twelve

SARAH ROHRER

1836-1860

First Southern Baptist Missionaries Appointed to Japan

"Are not five sparrows sold for two pennies? And not
one of them is forgotten before God." **Luke 12:6**

T he white oak deck of the clipper ship was stained with many
tears from the painful parting. Sarah, aged twenty-four, was an
only child and had been raised exclusively by her devoted mother
since her military father's death when Sarah was only nine. The
day of departure was August 3, 1860, from the Sandy Hook Harbor
in New Jersey. Sarah and her husband John had been married for
only three short months. This was supposed to be a time of smiles
and bright hopes. Why the departure? Why the tears?

John Quincy Adams Rohrer had surrendered his life several
years before to the call of God to be a missionary. He was willing
to go wherever the need was greatest. It was eventually decided
by the Foreign Mission Board in Richmond, Virginia, that John
should initiate Southern Baptist work in the great empire of Japan.

The US Navy had opened Japan to outside trade and contact
only a few years earlier. The spiritual need was great, and the door

was open. Now was the time to act. Now was the time to enter the Land of the Rising Sun to tell them of the Son of Righteousness, who had risen with healing in His wings.

In 1859, the Foreign Mission Board (SBC) appointed three single men for Japan, and the first to get married would be the first to go. John Rohrer was the first blessed to find a godly wife, Sarah Robinson, who shared a commitment to follow the command of Christ to make disciples of all nations. Four years before their departure, Sarah had made a public profession of faith and was baptized into the fellowship of a Baptist congregation in Montrose, Pennsylvania. She decided to become a Baptist, not because of family history, but through personal study of the New Testament. Before her baptism, she asked the church to pray that she would know clearly what Christ required of her. She wanted God to direct her in the path of her duty to Him. God did, and Sarah gladly obeyed. She was soon known as a faithful and devout member of that local assembly.

Sarah Robinson Rohrer was a remarkable young woman. Not only did she possess a keen and personal faith in Jesus Christ, but also she was highly educated, with an emphasis in music and languages. She had completed advanced studies in classical piano and bass and had been employed for several years teaching music to other young women. Her mother was eager for Sarah to continue using her musical skills, so she arranged for Sarah's piano and bass to be shipped to Japan. Sarah hoped to use her abilities as a platform for sharing Christ in her new home on the mission field. After her marriage to John, they briefly united with the First Baptist Church of Baltimore under the pastoral ministry of Rev. John Williams.

Finally, all preparations had been made, and passage was booked on a clipper ship *The Edwin Forest,* which was named for the most famous American actor of that era. They shared the journey with another Southern Baptist missionary couple, Alfred and Helena Bond, who were bound for Shanghai. These young people planned to travel first to Hong Kong and then to their respective fields of service.

Sarah's mother, Mrs. Robinson, joined her daughter and John in New York City to accompany them to the sailing vessel. She wrote, "When we alighted from the carriage at the wharf, I felt a strangeness like death, like having my heart torn out." She was overwhelmed with regret for consenting to Sarah's leaving with John. Mrs. Robinson said, "I gazed upon her with a begrudging eye and if it had been in my power I would have clutched her away from all the surroundings and fled with her in my arms into the wilderness. But I was powerless." She pulled Sarah aside, fell to her knees, and asked Sarah to forgive her for agreeing to this separation. Here is a mother pleading with her only daughter not to go. How did Sarah respond to this fervent plea?

Sarah and John stayed true to their calling and sailed away that night on a mission to reach Japan for Christ. Mrs. Robinson's final view of Sarah and John was of the couple, standing arm in arm at the railing, waving goodbye to her in the full moonlight. The anchor was raised, and the ship sailed away.... They were never heard from again! *The Edwin Forrest* and all its passengers were lost at sea. No one but the LORD knows what happened to them. It would be sixteen agonizing months before all hope was lost, and a memorial service was held in Baltimore for the Rohrers and the Bonds.

In the months after their departure, America changed forever. The Civil War broke out in April of 1861, and Southern Baptists were forced to postpone indefinitely all plans to enter Japan. Sadly, almost thirty years would elapse before Baptists in the South would try again. Precious time was lost, and a crucial window of opportunity closed. More than 165 years after the Rohrers were lost at sea, Japan remains largely unreached. Only one percent of Japan's more than 100 million people profess to be Christians. Japan still needs to meet the Savior.

The Rohrers never arrived. Never preached one sermon. Never sang one song. Never led one person to Christ. Even their own denomination barely remembers they ever existed. They have been forgotten. Their lives seem to have been fruitless. They sank before they started. What could God have been thinking?

Even though they were never heard from again, we can hear what Sarah said to her mother on that day of departure in August 1860. As Mrs. Robinson begged her daughter not to go to Japan, Sarah looked at her and said, *"Mother, with the exception of parting from you, this is the happiest day of my life, if we are lost at sea, death will find us in the path of duty."*

Such a life was not fruitless; the greatest battle had already been won. Sarah had fully and happily surrendered all to Jesus. She died in the path of obedience and with one quick step crossed the finish line into the joy of her Master. As Christians, we do not fail when our goals for Jesus are not reached. We fail when we do not fully surrender our goals to Jesus. Are you on the path of duty to Christ? Or are you on the path of duty to self?

In God's mysterious ways of working, Sarah's life and death still bear fruit. If Sarah's commitment inspires you to step onto the path of obedience to Christ, then that would be great fruit. Sarah is not forgotten by God, and maybe Sarah will not be forgotten by you. Though her body lies lost in the depths of the ocean, she speaks a better word to us than many who have lived long lives of ease and earthly success. If this were your last day, would you be found in the path of duty?

Solomon Ginsberg, missionary to Brazil

Chapter Thirteen

SOLOMON GINSBURG

1867-1927

Unlikely Southern Baptist Missionary to Brazil

"But he was pierced for our transgressions; he was crushed for our iniquities; upon him was the chastisement that brought us peace, and with his wounds we are healed." **Isaiah 53:5**

The impact of Solomon L. Ginsburg as a missionary for Jesus Christ is breathtaking! He served in Brazil for thirty-seven years, from 1890-1927, and died at only fifty-nine years of age. Ginsburg preached widely over the vast Brazilian territory and led thousands to faith in Christ. He planted churches, wrote and edited religious tracts and articles, and composed and translated numerous hymns for worship. His autobiography *A Wandering Jew in Brazil* is an exciting and engaging story of missionary adventure.

Ginsburg married a Southern Baptist missionary, Emma Morton, of Kansas City, Missouri, in 1893, following the unexpected death of his English bride. Although he had only recently affiliated with Southern Baptists, his union to Emma deepened his ties to the denomination. Together, they worked to reach Brazil for Christ.

He often preached in the open air, gathering a crowd by unfolding his ever-present Bilhorn organ and belting out a Gospel song in Portuguese. One of his favorites ran like this, *"Oh, the blood of Jesus cleansed me, Oh, the blood of Jesus cleansed me, Happily will I sing praises to my King, To my Lord Jesus, who saved me!"* In the early years, opposition to his preaching was intense. On more than one occasion, it landed him in jail. Once, his preaching even resulted in a "hit" being ordered on his life. The bandit, who came to kill him, was so overwhelmed by Solomon's gracious spirit that he repented of his evil intent and eventually became a believer.

In 1911, Pastor Solomon challenged the believers in one state of Brazil to pray and work for a thousand new converts to be baptized during that year. By God's grace, they reached their goal. He challenged his Baptist brothers and sisters to make the following three resolutions:

- To **speak** to some unsaved soul at least once every day.
- To **pray** every day at noon for the conversion of that person.
- To **give** a Bible or New Testament to every neighbor in whose home no Bible or New Testament was to be found.

All of Ginsburg's fruit *for* Christ is marvelous, but his conversion *to* Christ is even more amazing! Ginsburg was born to Jewish parents near Suwalki, Poland (which was under Russian control at that time) on the sixth day of August 1867. His father was a Jewish rabbi, who intended for Solomon to follow in his steps. After years of studying in his mother's hometown, Solomon returned to his parents at the age of fourteen. His father had arranged his marriage to the twelve-year-old daughter of a wealthy Jewish family. Solomon rebelled at that idea. He fled his home, never to see his parents again. Eventually, he made his way to London to live and work with one of his uncles, who owned a store in the East End.

Soon after his arrival, he met a missionary on the street from the Mildmay Mission to the Jews. The man asked him to come and hear him speak about Isaiah 53. Usually, Solomon would have rejected such an offer, but an incident that had taken place before he left his home in Poland compelled him to hear what this man had to say.

A few years before coming to London, Solomon's father had erected his customary tent near their house for the Feast of Tabernacles. This "booth" served as a place of discussion for the men of the community. In the tent, young Solomon found a copy of the book of Isaiah and began to read where it fell open to these words, *"He was pierced for our transgressions; he was crushed for our iniquities; upon him was the chastisement that brought us peace, and with his wounds we are healed."*

As Solomon began to ponder the meaning of the passage, he saw a handwritten note in the margin of the chapter, "to whom does the prophet refer?" Solomon had never considered the question, and he innocently posed it to his father, who looked surprised but remained silent. Solomon repeated the question and was shocked when his father angrily slapped him across the face. Solomon said, *"I felt quite chagrined and humiliated and I confess I did not like that kind of an answer—but in the Providence of God, it served its purpose, for, when that Jewish Missionary asked me to go and hear him explain that very same chapter I could not but remember that*

135

scene in the tent and, of course, went, out of curiosity to see if he had a better explanation to give than the one my father had given."

This seemingly random encounter with the Jewish missionary was the turning point in Solomon's life. The missionary showed him that Jesus is the one to whom Isaiah is referring. Solomon began to read the New Testament and was overwhelmed by the *"wonders of the life of the Messiah and how every prophecy was fulfilled in Jesus."* He was soon *"convinced that the Son of Mary, the crucified One, was the Christ of God, the Messiah of Israel, the Rejected One of my people."* Solomon exclaimed, *"It was not long after this that I realized I must cast in my lot with Jesus and plead for forgiveness for the part I had in that great crime of Calvary."*

In the early years after his conversion, Solomon experienced great persecution and rejection from his own people in London. God used these sufferings to make him into the bold witness for Jesus Christ that he would be in Brazil. During that time, he learned the printing trade through an occupational training ministry of the Mildmay Mission to the Jews, and he used that skill throughout his life as a missionary. Solomon knew the power of the printed word, especially the power of "The Word." What brought him to Christ was not the authority of man's word but the authority of God's Word. He heard God speaking through the Bible, and he knew that was what the people of Brazil needed to hear as well.

Throughout Solomon Ginsberg's ministry in Brazil, the Bible was always central. Solomon recounted the story of a poor mail carrier that trusted Christ as his Savior:

During his life as a slave, his legs had been hurt and he walked knock-kneed. To deliver the mail he walked a distance of about 75 miles. Soon after his conversion he asked me to teach him to read. He was about 50 years old. "Why do you want to learn to read?" I asked him. He replied, "First, because I want to read with my own eyes the letter of my Father in Heaven; then also, as I walk along the road delivering mail from farm to farm, I should like to be able to deliver my Father's letter to all that do not know him yet."

Solomon taught him to read, and the mail carrier used this ability in the farmhouses where he would spend the night on his route. He would read a passage aloud to everyone in the home, opening a door to witness for Christ.

Solomon's life shows us that God is ultimately guiding our steps. The fiercest trials we face *today* are preparing us for fruitful service *tomorrow*. God takes the strands of His children's lives and weaves them together into something beautiful and useful. This is especially evident when his children are humbly devoted to His purpose of bringing the Good News of salvation in Jesus Christ to the world.

Solomon Ginsberg for Brazil

Solomon Ginsberg at his desk

Printing shop of the Mildmay Mission to the Jews

Solomon Ginsberg

Erik Alfred Nelson, missionary to the Amazon

Chapter Fourteen

ERIK NELSON

1862-1939

Pioneer of Baptist Missions in the Amazon

"Getting into one of the boats, which was Simon's,
he asked him to put out a little from the land.
And he sat down and taught the people from the
boat."   **Luke 5:3**

E rik Alfred Nelson was a remarkable Southern Baptist pioneer
missionary. How that came to pass is astounding. In the words
of his first biographer, *"Erik Nelson fitted no man-made require-
ments for his task as a missionary to the Amazon Valley of Brazil."*
He finished only a few grades in school. He was not ordained until
he had been in the Amazon for five years. He had no formal medical knowledge to combat the myriad of tropical diseases he faced
over decades on the river. Additionally, he was born in Sweden and
baptized a Lutheran; he was not born in the Southern USA into a
Baptist family. God was most certainly the pilot of Nelson's life.

Erik was born in Örebro, Sweden, on December 17, 1862. His
parents were Anders and Annie Marie Nelson. Even though Anders
agreed to Erik's infant baptism, he himself was not part of the

Lutheran Church. He was a hard-working farmer, who turned his rocky patch of land, sixty miles inland from Stockholm, into a productive farm. Young Erik attended school for a couple of years, and one of his teachers was a Baptist, who shared his faith with Erik's father. The teacher's testimony had a profound impact on Anders. Not long after, when a traveling Bible salesman (also a Baptist) passed through the area, Anders requested to be baptized. Baptists were a despised group and outlawed by the Lutheran-controlled government in Sweden during that era. The Bible salesman, who baptized Anders, was whipped, his leg was broken, and he was thrown into a river to drown. However, the water revived him, and he managed to swim to safety.

Erik's father was aware of the dangers of being a Baptist; yet, he was so convinced and committed to biblical faith that he organized a Sunday school in his home. It quickly grew into a church. Eventually, Anders became a Baptist preacher. The persecution was so intense that many Swedish Baptists immigrated to America in search of religious freedom. Anders led his family and a group of three hundred to seek refuge in the USA.

Their westward migration ended in Chanute, Kansas, where Anders began a new life farming corn, oats, and wheat. Young Erik was responsible for the cattle, and he took them out on the prairie during the day. Erik loved the outdoors! His experiences in nature were very spiritually powerful for him, but he took no other interest in the things of God until he turned fourteen. He was converted during a revival and baptized by his father on April 10, 1877. Even though Erik trusted Christ as his Savior, his faith was not yet vitally important to him.

For the next eight years, he worked on his father's farm. When he turned twenty-two, the call of adventure drew him farther west to become a cowboy. He joined numerous cattle drives and eventually worked for the Santa Fe Railroad. He, along with many others, saw that the era of the open range in the Western United States was coming to an end. He heard of the great cattle country in northern Brazil near the Rio Branco, and Erik dreamed of owning a big ranch there. This dream did not come to pass, but it served to plant a seed of awareness in Erik's mind about the vast country to the south—Brazil.

Erik returned to Kansas and to his faith. He began reading his Bible with renewed interest and believed that God was calling him to preach. He was impressed by God's command to Abram, *"Go out of your country unto a country which I will show unto you."* Erik felt God was speaking those very same words to him. While attending a meeting of the Swedish Baptist Association, a letter from "Buck" Bagby was read to the group. Bagby, a Southern Baptist pioneer missionary to Brazil, wrote of the desperate need of that country for the Gospel of Jesus Christ. This was a pivotal event for Erik, who sensed that God was leading him to Brazil. In preparation, Erik preached numerous revivals in Swedish Baptist Churches. In one of those revivals, he met Ida Wilhelmina Lundburg, who later became his wife. Erik took his small savings and booked passage to Belém, Brazil, at the mouth of the Amazon.

Upon his arrival in November 1891, Belém was racked by an epidemic of yellow fever. Erik got to work caring for crewmembers of the almost sixty ships in the harbor. This led to his first job as a chaplain to sailors. Any ship that raised the "Bethel flag" was to be the site of a service of worship. This provided Erik with practical ministry experience and gave him a toehold in Brazil. He wrote back to the USA and proposed to Ida. After accepting his proposal, this amazing woman came to meet him in Brazil, alone, and with no financial help. They were married on the day of her arrival.

Soon after their wedding, Ida fell ill with the yellow fever that was plaguing the city, but mercifully, she recovered. As a gifted seamstress, her skills provided much needed income for the family. In numerous other ways, she served a vital role in the establishment of their ministry in the Amazon. In later years, she fell seriously ill again, forcing her to return to the United States, but she insisted that her husband continue to fulfill his calling in Brazil. Her encouragement and support—despite long years of separation—resulted in the salvation of many. Eternity will surely reward her temporal sacrifices.

Erik continued ministering to international sailors in the Belém harbor, but as he learned Portuguese, his desire increased to reach Brazilians living up the Amazon River. He began his ministry on the Amazon as a Bible salesman (colporteur). This gave the Brazilians what they needed and did not have: the Word of God; it gave Erik what he needed and did not have: income and language acquisition.

Erik's Bibles cost thirty-five cents, which was five times cheaper than if purchased in a bookstore. He sold them in the markets, on the street corners, and on the steamships that traveled up and down the mighty Amazon. Many people bought Bibles, and many more persecuted him for selling them. Thrown in jail, mobbed, and threatened, Erik was forced to flee for his life on numerous occasions. Despite his ill treatment, Erik never grew bitter against the Brazilians. He knew they were prejudiced against Protestants and the Bible by their upbringing and training in the Roman Catholic Church. Erik grew in his love for the Brazilians and was pained by the idolatrous practices which marked their religious lives. The Bible was withheld from them. The Gospel was withheld from them. And ultimately, Jesus the Savior was withheld from them. This broke his heart.

Erik preached and preached and preached; yet few, very few, believed during those early years. He seriously considered giving up. His wife pleaded with him to pray and ask God to change his heart. He refused, saying it would do no good. She insisted and pressed him to realize that either Jesus or Satan was going to win the victory in him that day. Finally, his heart softened, and he fell to his knees and asked God to strengthen him in the face of persistent opposition and lack of visible fruitfulness. That day God won the victory in his heart. He learned, never to forget again, that *"God does not follow man's plans—that the missionary's business is to preach the Gospel, live a pure life, and leave the results to God."*

Year after year, Erik continued to distribute Bibles and to preach whenever he had an opportunity. He wrote to Southern Baptist missionary, Solomon Ginsburg, and asked him to make a trip north to help constitute the first Baptist church in the Amazon. Ginsburg came, and the First Baptist Church of Belém, Brazil, was established on February 2, 1897. Ginsburg recognized Nelson's great evangelistic heart, aided him to be ordained as a Baptist pastor, and recommended him as a missionary candidate to the Foreign Mission Board of the Southern Baptist Convention. The Board accepted Solomon's recommendation, and Erik Alfred Nelson became a Southern Baptist missionary.

147

The Nelsons moved almost one thousand miles up the Amazon River. The city of Manaus became their headquarters and the center of Baptist work throughout the Amazon Valley. They planted the first Baptist Church in that city, but Erik was never a person to be limited to one place and one congregation. He was a true *apostolic* missionary. At first, he traveled wherever the steamships would take him, but he was not content to pass by hundreds of villages and homes that were untouched by the Gospel. He bought a canoe and paddled over seven hundred miles preaching to thousands along the way. His "parish" was a territory of over three million square miles. He fell seriously ill on numerous occasions and was told by the doctor to give up his river travels. He refused, believing the open air to be his best cure.

He appealed for other workers to join him in this enormous mission field. Erik argued that merchants from all over the world came to the waters of the Amazon seeking to make a few paltry dollars, but Christians, who had the message of salvation and life, closed their ears and hearts to the lost of that region because it was *too* hot, *too* hard, and *too* isolated. He pled over and over again, *"Who will come and help us?"*

Slowly, but surely, people began to listen and were converted to Christ. Years of sowing turned into decades of reaping. One convert, a carpenter, built Erik an uncovered boat, larger than the canoe, and operated by an outboard motor. He named it *Noah's Ark*. This helped Erik extend his ministry but was inadequate for long and dangerous trips up the Amazon and its tributaries. The Nelsons prayed for an adequate ministry vessel. In 1919, the First Baptist Church of Murray, Kentucky, gave $3,000 to build the much-needed boat. The result was one of the first oil-burning launches

on the Amazon, and it served the Nelsons for the next twe
It was called *The Buffalo*. Nelson's biographer says, *"Th_ _ _ _ _ _ _,
Kentucky, church will know only in eternity how many people will
meet them and call them blessed for giving of the launch to that
vast field."* One hundred years later, that church continues significant support of Gospel ministry in the Amazon.

After three decades of missionary service, Erik wrote, *"The
Amazon valley is not a paradise, but thirty-odd years ago God sent
me here and he has held me up, using your prayers and means; I
am still alive. The only place of danger is the place of disobedi-
ence...Send us men and women who will come because they cannot
stay away!"* Erik was often the only Christian worker that visited
the thousands of people living along the banks of the rivers and
lakes of Amazonia. He was greatly loved by them all. He led many
to Christ and organized numerous churches.

Finally, he was forced to retire, and he returned to the USA in
1936, after more than forty years in Brazil. Curiously, the Pilot of
his life was not finished with him. Erik had never become a citizen
of the United States and had to leave the country. He returned to
Brazil alone, but with the blessings of Ida, and served there until his
death in 1939. He was buried in Manaus, and thousands attended
his funeral.

Shortly before his death, Erik took a younger missionary with
him to visit many of the Christians and churches that had resulted
from his ministry. That missionary was Lewis Malen Bratcher, who
authored the inspiring biography of Erik Nelson *The Apostle of the
Amazon*. On that final journey, they met for worship with a group
of Japanese immigrants on the banks of Lake Maues. Bratcher
wrote that the group said the Lord's Prayer together. Bratcher

spoke English; Erik, Swedish; the Brazilians, Portuguese; and the immigrants from Japan prayed in Japanese. Nelson was known for his booming voice, which was so well suited for preaching out of doors. At the end of that multi-ethnic service, they sang, *"God be with you till we meet again...till we meet, till we meet at Jesus' feet."* Erik's voice rang out loud and clear. It was his last song here on earth. On the return trip to Manaus, he fell ill, and not long after arriving in that city, he died.

After the funeral, Bratcher felt compelled to travel to as many congregations as possible to share with them that Nelson had passed into glory. In every congregation, Bratcher was deeply touched by the outpourings of love and appreciation for Erik Nelson. One conversation about Nelson, representative of hundreds, went as follows, "He was my spiritual father. If it had not been for him, I would still be in the darkness and ignorance of a mistaken religion. It cannot be true that he is gone—that he will never again go out and tell others about the Master. Who will care for the people of the Amazon Valley, now that Nelson has gone?"

Who indeed?

*The two photographs that follow are:
Riverboat in the Amazon
Erik and Ida Nelson

Erik Nelson

Erik Nelson

Nelson's Motor Boat on the Amazon.
(Showing River 800 miles from its mouth.)

Erik Nelson in his motorboat

The Buffalo in a far-flung lake of the Amazon

Eric Nelson preparing for a 1,500 mile journey up the Amazon

George Holcombe Lacy, missionary to Mexico

Chapter Fifteen

GEORGE LACY

1868-1949

Theological Educator and Faithful Sufferer in Mexico

"When Jesus had finished instructing his twelve disciples, he went on from there to teach and preach in
their cities."   **Matthew 11:1**

G eorge Holcombe Lacy was born into a strong Presbyterian
family with several generations of distinguished pastors
and teachers. His grandfather had been a pioneer Presbyterian
pastor, who started many congregations in Missouri, Tennessee,
and Arkansas. He and his wife started the first school in El Dorado,
Arkansas, in 1846 and planted four Presbyterian churches.

George's father, Captain Watson Lacy, distinguished himself as
a soldier. He fought in the first battle of Bull Run near Manassas,
Virginia, in 1861. In the following year at the Battle of Shiloh,
when all of the officers of his regiment were killed, Jefferson Davis
commissioned him as an officer for his gallantry. Captain Lacy survived the war and returned home to El Dorado in 1865. He married
Sallie Holcombe and bought one hundred and twenty acres to begin
farming. Their first child, George, was born on October 13, 1868.

At nineteen, George left the farm and traveled to Texas. In March of 1888, he was converted to Christ in Lamar County, Texas, and joined the Presbyterian Church. With only fifteen dollars in his pocket, George made his way to Arkansas College (Lyon College), a Presbyterian-affiliated school in Batesville, Arkansas. Upon completion of his degree in 1892, he enrolled in Columbia Presbyterian Seminary, which was then located in Columbia, South Carolina. George, a good student, who enjoyed learning, had deep and meaningful ties to the Presbyterian denomination.

He married Minnie Lou Meek, eleven years his junior, on October 5, 1893. Both of Minnie's parents had died when she was a child; during that time of sadness, she trusted Christ as her Savior. She joined the Three Creeks Baptist Church at the age of fifteen. After their marriage, the Lacys moved to South Carolina for seminary.

While attending Presbyterian Seminary, George's study of Scripture continued to raise doubts in his mind about the validity of infant baptism and other related doctrines. He completed seminary in 1895 and was ordained to the Presbyterian ministry. His doubts only intensified until he decided that he could no longer embrace Presbyterianism. He was convinced that the Bible's teaching about conversion, baptism, church membership, and religious liberty was best expressed by the Baptists; so, he became one! Consequently, he wrote *Why I Became a Baptist*, a book that expounds his reasons for taking this difficult, but compelling, step.

The Lacys moved to Southwest Texas where George began his ministry as a Baptist pastor by serving congregations in the little towns of Kennedy and Gonzales. The church in Gonzales granted him a leave of absence to attend Southern Seminary in Louisville for a session of advanced study in Greek, Hebrew, and theology. George possessed the greatest trait of a teacher; he was a life-long learner.

From these South Texas towns, not far from the Mexican border, George and Minnie accepted a call to Mexico as Southern Baptist missionaries. In May of 1903, they arrived at their new field of service in Saltillo, Mexico, with their four children: Sallie Meek, Julia, Eula, and their only boy, Watson Eldridge. Several months later, they were delighted to welcome their fifth child, Octavia.

The Madero Institute had been started by Southern Baptist missionaries in 1884 and gave many Mexican girls a wonderful Christian education. They learned reading and writing, Bible, skills for home, and skills for the workplace. This was a most unique institution in a land where women did not have many educational opportunities. Additionally, the school gave many orphans a safe and loving home, as well as an excellent education. The school closed in 1898, after fourteen years of service, because of internal conflicts among the missionary staff and faculty.

George's primary assignment in Mexico was to reopen the Madero Institute. It took Lacy six months to gather the necessary teachers; the school reopened on January 11, 1904. Within two months, they had an enrollment of fifty girls. George's family lived in the school, and though they were surrounded by the bustle of it all, it must have been a great environment for the five young Lacy children.

On December 28, 1904, all was quiet in the Lacy home because the girls from the school were away on Christmas break. After eighteen months as missionaries, George and Minnie were settling into their new life in Saltillo. He had recently baptized seven new converts and was enthusiastic about their progress. Little did they know what the next fifteen days would hold.

Their baby, Octavia, became sick that day and within twelve hours was dead. Then, their only boy, Watson Eldridge, fell ill with the same symptoms, and three days later he also died. George hurriedly put Minnie and the three remaining children on a train headed back to his family home in Arkansas. On the journey, all three children became sick and died. Minnie was forced to stop along the way to bury them.

Shockingly, all five were now dead. It appears to have been scarlet fever that took the lives of their children in such a quick and violent way.

George followed Minnie on the next train, only to learn the devastating news upon his arrival. Later, as they stood by the graveside of the children who died on the way, George said, *"My Dear, we will give up and come home."*

But Minnie replied, ***"No, we have given our children for Mexico, and now we will go back and give our lives."***

George wrote to the board in Richmond to tell them of their unimaginable loss. He said, *"Sometimes it seems like more than we can bear...."*

Yet, with bleeding hearts, they returned to Mexico. In a turn of God's providence, reminiscent of Job, five more children were born to Minnie and George; four would live into adulthood.

Over the next several years, they served in various places in Mexico (Saltillo, Toluca, and Torreon), and everywhere they went, George was a teacher. He taught women who became teachers, mothers, and secretaries—even the secretary to one of the presidents of Mexico. He taught men, who became Sunday school teachers and pastors. He taught Bible, Greek, Hebrew, and philosophy. Whatever needed to be taught, George Lacy taught!

The Mexican Revolution started in 1910 and lasted through 1920. Almost all of the missionaries left during those years, but the Lacys remained. George had many close calls with death. Once, when George ventured out of his house in Lerdo, a musket ball barely missed his head and buried itself in the adobe wall behind him. In another close call, bandits robbed George and stole all of his money. Worst of all, the Baptist Theological Institute in Torreon was ransacked in a terrifying attack described by George:

> *Yes, I was there when they poured the fire into our houses and I am here yet. Our school was completely sacked from top to bottom. Nothing was left but the buildings.... Thirteen Chinamen were killed around our schoolhouse. Over two hundred were killed in the city. I never want to see such sights again. Monday afternoon they were in the streets in piles.*

George ministered comfort and encouragement to the believers in the La Laguna region during the revolution. He visited isolated congregations to let them know they were not forgotten. He prayed with young Baptist men, who were conscripted to fight in the conflict. When the young men asked Lacy if he were afraid to stay, he said he was not afraid because God was with him. These years of quiet solidarity with the Mexican people won George their undying admiration and love. He increasingly identified himself with Mexican believers and their struggles. For a short period near the end of the revolution, all missionaries were entirely forced out of Mexico. The Lacys left Mexico, but George continued to work for its conversion to Christ from the Baptist Publishing House in EL Paso. He edited *El Expositor Bíblico* and shipped it across the border into Mexico.

At the end of the war, the Lacys returned to Mexico, and George returned to teaching. He continued to serve Christ in this capacity for many years. Minnie, who was worn out after bearing ten children and experiencing immense grief, broke down entirely and died at the age of fifty-six in 1933. George continued to serve as a missionary for two more years until he reached the mandatory retirement age of seventy.

What did George do in retirement? He returned to Mexico and taught the Bible far and wide. He started a mobile Bible institute and traveled throughout the country, training Sunday school teachers and pastors, who had little access to such learning. George continued this itinerant ministry for the next eleven years. He was a beloved patriarch of the Mexican Baptist churches. He fully identified with them, and when speaking of Mexicans, George always began his sentences with "we Mexicans." Finally, on November 27, 1949, the Lord called George home. This faithful servant was eighty-one years of age and had given forty-six years of his life as a missionary teacher to Mexico.

The Bible School he started continues today in the southern Mexican state of Oaxaca as Seminario Teológico Bautista Lacy. After more than eighty years, Seminario Lacy remains faithful to its founder's vision of training God-called ministers, missionaries, pastors, and teachers. The life and struggles of the Lacys continue to inspire and challenge each new generation of students. The school awards five scholarships, which are given in memory of the Lacy children,* who died in the path of their parents' obedience to the call of Christ upon their lives.

When George died, his friends entered the humble room where he lived and were brought to tears. This spiritual giant of a man, who had taught generations of pastors and teachers, had only a few earthly possessions. He ate his meals on *campesino* plates and drank from simple adobe mugs. He had become one with them, so they could become one with Christ.

*The five Lacy children who died:
Octavia, 14 months
Watson Eldridge, 3 years and 4 months
Eula, 6 years
Julia, 8 years
Sallie Meek, 10 years and 5 months

MR. & MRS. G. H. LACY AND FAMILY, 1904.

The Lacy family

George Lacy

T.W. Ayers, medical missionary to North China

Chapter Sixteen

T.W. AYERS

1858-1954
Pioneer Medical Missionary

"Whenever you enter a town and they receive you,
eat what is set before you. Heal the sick in it and
say to them, 'The kingdom of God has come near
to you.'"   **Luke 10:8-9**

D octor Ayers prayed as never before. He cried out to God to
make the woman breathe. This was the tensest moment of
his life. Perspiration poured down his face. If this lady died, the
new medical mission would be over before it started. In the tiny
makeshift operating room, Dr. Ayers pled with God *for the sake of
the Lord Jesus Christ who died to save these poor people to make
her breathe.* At that moment, the woman took a deep breath, but
only one. Ayers cried out, *"Oh, God, make her do it again!"* She
took a few irregular breaths and then began to breathe more nor-
mally. Ayers knew the Great Physician had just worked a miracle.

This was the first surgery performed by Dr. Thomas Wilburn
Ayers in Hwanghsien, China, in 1901. Earlier that day, a wealthy
Chinese man dressed in an expensive silk suit had entered the crude,

10'x15' room converted for use as a medical office and dispensary. Walking behind the man was a small, pale woman supported by a servant. The wealthy Chinese man said she was his *little wife* (concubine), she had an abscess in her cheek that had erupted with offensive pus, and he wanted the doctor to cut it out immediately.

Dr. Ayers examined the woman and discovered she had "*a necrosed jaw bone*" that needed to be removed; however, they were not equipped for surgeries. They did not even have an operating table. Only a few days before, the tiny medical office had been the gatekeeper's house with dirt everywhere and walls blackened with soot. Dr. Ayers had cleaned and sanitized the room to the best of his ability, but it was far from being ready. Although the Chinese man insisted on surgery that very day, Dr. Ayers declined and listed the many reasons it would be unwise. However, Ayers' heart was moved deeply when the sick woman informed him (through a female missionary interpreter) that her husband was planning to throw her out on the street if she did not have the surgery that day.

The missionary physician asked to be excused and walked over to the nearby house where he and his family were living. He found a little room, shut the door, and fell to his knees. Dr. Ayers poured out his heart to God and asked for guidance. Before he finished praying, God made the answer clear, *"Lose sight of yourself and try to help that woman."*

Ayers quickly located a wooden dining table to use for the operation. He washed everything in the room with an antiseptic solution and prepared his instruments and the anesthesia. He was glad he had three people, who could serve as surgical assistants: his interpreter, the female missionary, and his elderly language teacher. His interpreter was petrified and could only promise help with translation. The female missionary informed the doctor she also could offer no help beyond translating. Although he was disappointed, the doctor was grateful for God's provision. With his first incision, blood shot up, and the interpreter went down. At least he had the female missionary. He turned to see her, but she was gone. He called her name, and she responded through the window, saying the first whiff of chloroform was too much for her. Dr. Ayers, with his elderly language teacher standing at the foot of the table, performed the surgery.

The surgery went smoothly until the woman reacted to the anesthesia and stopped breathing. Ayers prayed, and God answered. The woman not only started breathing again but also made a full recovery. She returned home to live with her husband. The story of her operation and healing spread far and wide. In fact, Dr. Ayers estimated that at least 2,000 people came for treatment as a direct result of her story. Every one of those patients heard the Gospel of Jesus Christ, many of them for the first time.

T.W. Ayers had come to North China as a medical missionary of the Foreign Mission Board (SBC). He was born in Ayersville, Georgia, on December 22, 1858. Soon after his birth, his parents moved the family to Carnesville, Georgia, where T.W. was raised. His father was a merchant, but T.W. knew he was not cut out for that line of work. He had two interests as a young person: medicine and journalism. Ayers recalled, *"I felt so strongly that I should be a doctor that I went to Athens and bought a Grays Anatomy, which I often read at night. But my decision was not definite, for the field of journalism continued to appeal to me."*

T.W. trusted Christ as his Savior at the age of fifteen. As he prepared to be baptized and unite his life with the Cross Roads Baptist

Church, his parents expressed their desire to do the same. T.W. said, *"Up to this time my father and mother had not joined the church, though my mother had been a Christian for many years, she had waited for my father to become a Christian, so that they could join at the same time. My father was a moral and honest man but was so busy as a business man that he seemed to give little thought to religion, but my conversion so impressed him that he did all that was necessary to be saved, and he, my mother and I were baptized the same day in the creek near Carnesville."*

As an eighteen-year-old, T.W. bought a newspaper (*The Franklin County Register*) in Carnesville and quickly learned the ropes of writing articles and setting type. He was both the editor and publisher of this four-page, six-column, weekly paper. He bought the paper on credit but was so successful that he paid it off in a year and soon after sold it for twice what he paid for it. He bought a second newspaper (*The Sun)* in Hartwell, Georgia. There he married Minnie Skelton, and they began a family.

Ayers continued publishing his paper and took classes at the Medical College of Georgia in Augusta, but God was beginning a new work in his heart. Ayers remembered that at the age of twenty-four, *"while in Hartwell I had, in addition to the hands of medicine and journalism, another hand laid on me. I had an absolutely clear and definite call to give my life to God as a foreign missionary. This call so impressed me that I announced it publically the first Sunday after it came to me in the Baptist Church in Hartwell."* Ayers soon came to regret this public announcement because he was not fully ready to make the necessary sacrifices to follow Christ to the mission field. God's call would go unheeded for eighteen years.

In 1883, the Ayers family moved to Anniston, Alabama, where T.W. bought *The Daily Hot Blast,* a local paper, and he opened a drug store as well. His earnings from these businesses paid his tuition at the Baltimore College of Physicians and Surgeons where he completed his medical degree. He went into full-time medical practice in Anniston in 1886. Ayers became deeply rooted in Alabama life. He and Minnie had seven children during those years (two more were born later in China), and they were very involved in the ministry of Parker Memorial Baptist Church. Ayers was also active in the Alabama Baptist State Convention and more generally, in Alabama state politics, especially as president of the Good Roads Association.

Despite these wonderful endeavors, Ayers knew he was not fully obeying God. He wrote:

> *In all these years in medicine and journalism I never got away from that call to be a foreign missionary. The call was constantly coming to me, but never was the call so persistent as now. I saw the time of decision was at hand, and I went up into my office, locked the door, got down on my knees and turned to God to settle this question definitely. I pled with Him to make it clear as to whether I was to go or stay, and the answer came as clearly as if it had been an audible voice, saying, "Go". This settled it. I wrote a letter at once to Dr. R. J. Willingham, Secretary of the Foreign Mission Board of the Southern Baptist Convention, offering myself as a foreign medical missionary. I told him of my call,*

> *and said that I had fought this call so long that I*
> *was now forty-two years old, had a wife and seven*
> *children, which made it probably impossible for any*
> *Board to consider appointing me, but God had said*
> *to me go, and now to settle the question once and*
> *for always I was making this application.*

In his response, Secretary Willingham praised God for this direct answer to the prayers of thousands. Willingham explained that a missionary couple in North China had recently lost two little children to disease with no medical doctor available to assist them. Their situation had touched the hearts of Baptist women in Georgia, who quickly raised the funds to send a doctor and his family to China. The funds had to sit in the bank because no doctor could be found who was willing to go.

They decided there was only one way to solve their problem—Prayer! They planned a gathering and invited Secretary Willingham to join them. In his first letter to Ayers, Willingham shared a stunning detail, *"as well as I can reckon the time, while you were on your knees in your office settling the question of surrendering yourself to God's will, I was in Savannah, Ga., and with a large number of Georgia women was on my knees praying God to thrust out a doctor who would make the sacrifice to go in answer to this appealing need."* Ayers trembled as he read this letter. God was orchestrating this entire circumstance!

When Ayers filled out his official application, he requested a reference from one of the most important leaders among Alabama Baptists. The leader responded that God would never call a man to make such an extreme sacrifice. Ayers thought this letter signaled the closing of the door, but a week later, both Ayers and Willingham received a second letter from the man. He was ashamed of his former lack of faith in God, exclaiming, "THERE IS NO SACRIFICE IN ALL THIS WORLD TOO GREAT FOR A MAN TO MAKE FOR THE LORD JESUS CHRIST."

According to Ayers, the motivating force in his missionary call was the Bible. As Dr. Ayers read, *"he caught a wonderful vision of the Master as He went from place to place in Palestine, showing forth His compassion by healing the sick and suffering. He saw Him everywhere putting love into action. He saw that the Master had given an example of healing and preaching."*

As the Ayers family was preparing to leave for the field, China exploded in a violent hatred of foreigners and all who were associated with them. The Boxer Rebellion began in Shantung where the Ayers were assigned to work. Almost 250 foreign missionaries and approximately 15,000 Chinese Christians were murdered during this hostility. Undaunted, the Ayers arrived in May of 1901 as the uprising was quelled; however, all missionaries were still taking refuge in coastal cities. From Chefoo (Yentai) the Ayers family was transported sixty miles by oxcart with a military escort to the city of Hwanghsien.

Ayers studied Chinese during the morning and saw patients in the afternoon. Missionaries are usually expected to devote the first couple of years exclusively to language learning. Ayers asked to be an exception to the practice because he was 42 years old, and people needed medical attention right then. Dr. Ayers was marked by unfailing courtesy, compassion, and skill; in short order, his little examining room was overflowing with patients. Eight months later, the first trained Southern Baptist missionary nurse, Miss

Jessie Pettigrew, arrived. She was a tireless worker, who greatly strengthened and expanded the medical ministry.

As the number of patients grew, Ayers prayed that God would provide the funds to build a proper hospital. The First Baptist Church of Macon, Georgia, responded to the need and sent $3,000 to build the first Southern Baptist hospital outside the USA. Ayers eagerly set about overseeing the construction process, and in 1903, the Warren Memorial Hospital opened to receive patients. It was named in memory of a beloved former pastor of the Macon church, Rev. E.W. Warren. The hospital continued to attract both poor and rich to its healing environs. The number of women coming on an annual basis was so high that the Baptist women of Georgia donated the funds to build a separate building and named it the Ayers Hospital for Women.

As much as Ayers loved being a doctor, he loved being an evangelist even more. He recognized that the deepest need of a person is spiritual healing. He put the evangelistic work first, and he ensured the medical ministry was always closely tied to evangelism. He wrote:

> *Of the thousands who have come to this hospital for treatment, I think I can safely say that at least three-fourths of them are people who have never attended a service at any of our churches or chapels. All of these people who have come for treatment have heard the gospel, many of them gladly, and some of them have accepted Christ as their personal Savior.*

By 1911, the hospital was well established, and almost 13,000 patients came through its doors annually. That winter, a terrifying "pneumonic plague," carried by returning migrant workers, swept into Shandong from Manchuria. It killed thousands of people. It was a deadly disease, so mysterious that it was described as *"the pestilence that walketh in darkness."* Dr. Ayers and the staff of Warren Memorial hospital stepped into the chaos and provided vital leadership. Dr. Ayers recognized that no one who contracted the disease survived. He knew it was imperative to quarantine the sick, to detain new arrivals from Manchuria, and to prohibit all public gatherings. These thoughtful measures slowed the spread of the disease, and by the time warmer weather arrived, the plague was fully contained.

However, a political storm followed immediately in its wake. The Chinese revolted against the Manchu Dynasty and its government. Every region and city had its own battles between those in support of the Manchus and the revolutionaries calling for their overthrow. The city of Hwanghsien was a bloody battleground, and the missionaries were forced to evacuate to the coast. Dr. Ayers was happy that his family was safe in Chefoo but worried about the hospital and its staff. Despite serious warnings not to return, Ayers traveled back to the hospital.

When he arrived, he realized the hospital was right in the middle of the war zone. He was surprised to find an elderly American lady wandering through the wards ministering comfort and sharing Christ with the patients: Lottie Moon! Ayers convinced her that she should not stay, but how could they get her out of the city safely? Ayers hastily organized the first branch of the Red Cross in Hwanghsien. Under the Red Cross, Lottie Moon was allowed to leave the city in safety. Lottie Moon was not the only beneficiary; wounded soldiers on both sides of the conflict received much needed help under this new shield of protection.

While dealing with these crises, Ayers received a desperate message from Chefoo that his wife had fallen ill and was dying. Though it was the middle of the night, he hurriedly set out to reach her and was attacked by robbers on the journey. When the robbers realized who he was, they returned all of his things, begged forgiveness, and urged him to continue on his way (Ayers had cared for many of them at the hospital). Mrs. Ayers survived but struggled with poor health for the rest of her life.

After a furlough, the Ayers returned to Hwanghsien and continued to serve there until 1926 when Minnie's failing health forced them to leave China for the final time. Ayers not only had treated thousands of patients, but also had trained numerous Chinese doctors to carry on the work. Above all, Ayers had pointed everyone to the Great Physician, who heals body *and* soul. After his departure, the city of Hwanghsien honored him (only one of two living men) with a public monument in the city; it reads, "He treated poor and rich alike."

A few years later Minnie died, but T.W. lived until he was 95 years old. *Healing and Missions*, his book about Southern Baptist medical work, included his personal experiences. It inspired many to become missionaries, one of whom was a young doctor by the name of Bill Wallace. Ayers was active and energetic almost to the very end of his life. The last question he ever asked a visitor was, *"How's my church?"*

Although Ayers did much good and was greatly honored, he went to China, not to represent himself or Southern Baptists, but to represent Jesus Christ. This is best illustrated by an incident that occurred early in his missionary career. One morning Dr. Ayers was called to help a badly beaten man lying outside the hospital wall. A great crowd gathered to watch. Ayers knelt beside the man, cleaned his infected wounds, and gently bandaged them.

A Chinese teacher in the crowd, who was amazed at what he saw, enquired, "Do you tell me that he has knelt beside the body of this dirty, suffering man, that he has with his own hands washed his offensive wounds, and used all this medicine, cotton, and cloth and expects no money for it?"

A Chinese Christian standing beside Dr. Ayers affirmed that the assistance had been given freely, but he hastened to add, "I do not want you to make a mistake here this morning in the presence of all these men. If there is any honor to be given for the little act of love and service you have witnessed, then do not give it to this foreign doctor.... He has not stood here in his own shoes, but has stood here as a servant...if there is any credit to be accorded...give it to his Master, the Lord Jesus Christ, who sent him to China for this very purpose."

The non-Christian Chinese teacher had previously ignored every conversation about Christ. However, after seeing Dr. Ayers act with such love and compassion to a suffering stranger, he exclaimed, "Today I have seen something with my eyes and there is no opening in the back of my head for it to go out. I must confess to you that your Jesus religion is the only religion in the world that has ever sent a man forth to act as we have seen it here today...to help a man when he is friendless and suffering."

The witness of Dr. T.W. Ayers was so powerful because he stood in Jesus' shoes, not his own, and walked in Jesus' steps, ministering healing both to broken bodies and to sinful souls.

179

T.W. Ayers

Dr. Ayers with medals awarded to him by the Chinese government

Dr. Ayers with Chinese medical school graduates

Dr. Ayers with a young patient

Monument in North China honoring Dr. Ayers

William W. Enete Sr., missionary to Brazil

Chapter Seventeen

WILLIAM ENETE

1893-1967
Missionary Ventriloquist

"And the master said to the servant, 'Go out to the
highways and hedges and compel people to come
in, that my house may be filled.'"   **Luke 14:23**

William W. Enete Sr. had a most unique ministry among
Southern Baptist missionaries. Enete captivated the attention of countless audiences with his ventriloquist doll, Sammy. The
simple messages that came through Sammy were etched in the
memories of the hearers. Enete was not only a skilled ventriloquist,
but also he was a pioneer in the adoption of numerous creative technologies for evangelism: movies, illusion, and chalk talks. Enete
and his wife, who were affectionately known as Uncle Billy and
Aunt Crystal, shared the Gospel throughout the country of Brazil
for almost four decades using these innovative methods.

Enete was born in Jonesville, Louisiana, on November 26,
1893. He grew up learning many practical skills as he worked in a
blacksmith shop, a boat repair shop, and an automobile garage. He
became a Christian and was baptized at the age of fifteen. Over the

next six years, Enete built a successful auto repair business; yet, he sensed that God was calling him into another form of service. In 1914, at the age of twenty-one, Enete entered Louisiana College and in six years completed both his high school and college course work. While he was a student, he learned photography, printing, the art of illusion, and the basics of ventriloquism.

Dr. Godbold, who later became the president of Louisiana College, urged Enete to attend the Southern Baptist Theological Seminary in Louisville, Kentucky. During Enete's years at Southern, he began dating Crystal Armstrong from Mountain Grove, Missouri, who was a student at the Woman's Missionary Training School. Upon graduation, Crystal taught at Ewing College in Illinois while William returned to Louisiana to pastor a new church in Shreveport—Jewella Baptist Church—located in a growing area near the Libbey Glass manufacturing plant. Enete baptized a young man named Jimmie Davis, who went on to a notable career as a musician and politician. Davis twice served as the governor of Louisiana but is best known as the author of the beloved song "You are My Sunshine."

Both William and Crystal sensed that God was calling them to marriage and missions, both of which they embraced in whirl-wind fashion. They married in May of 1924, were appointed missionaries in July, sailed for the field in September, and arrived in Brazil in October—all in five months! They were now firmly set on their life path. Over the course of the next decade, God blessed them with four children: William Jr., Noble, Happy, and Joy. As they began to learn Portuguese, William Sr. started sharing the Gospel and experimenting with the creative methods for which he would become so well known. He was an early-adopter of new technologies, "and long before it was recognized generally that a missionary could contribute to the cause of missions through photography, Enete was lugging all kinds of photographic equipment to the field. It is said that Dr. Ray (FMB administrator) advised him to throw his camera in the Gulf of Mexico. However, he didn't let such opinions discourage him. He learned photography in the old school and taking top quality pictures through the use of glass plates and flash powder long before modern flash bulbs and films became available."

Enete was invited to assist with a Vacation Bible School (VBS) and found that he loved teaching children. He really wanted to grab their attention, so he spent time at the Baptist Publishing House in Rio de Janeiro using their excellent tools to fashion a doll to use for ventriloquism. He described the process, *"I nailed the nose on and hinged the lower jaw. The neck finished and a string attached, Johnny gave forth a cry of well being, much to the amazement of the interested onlookers. Mrs. S.L. Watson, a missionary and the mother of two small boys, furnished the clothing. And Johnny became a real person—at least to the children."*

During their first term of service in Brazil, Uncle Billy (Enete) used Johnny to help him teach important life lessons, such as honesty, respect, and obedience. Together, Uncle Billy and Johnny reviewed the Bible story that was taught at VBS each day and challenged the children to trust Jesus Christ as their Savior. Little did Uncle Billy know he had found his life's work!

While the Enetes were in the USA on their first furlough, a woman gave them a professionally made ventriloquist doll named Sammy. Sammy became Uncle Billy's constant companion for many decades, and they "traveled by car, steamship, canoe, riverboat, horse and muleback, oxcart, train and airplane." Sammy was a delightful missionary tool that introduced tens of thousands of people, especially children, to Jesus Christ. Enete was described as "a wandering evangelist who uses every trick in his extra large hat in order to attract and hold the attention of his listeners. His talking doll, Sammy, always a favorite attraction, is known by children all the way from Rio Grande do Sul to the Amazon Valley. His ever-present silver dollar, which has a habit of turning up in the most unexpected places, never fails to enhance his audience— whether it be made up of half a dozen children or a large crowd of friendly, curious Brazilians.... Missionary Enete's unique talents have opened many doors for the gospel. He is frequently asked to speak in public or Catholic schools."

William Enete reached many people through these creative means, but he received criticism of his methods as sensational and his content as simplistic. While it is true that the lessons were very simple, it is also true Enete reached people that no one else was reaching. He got the message of Christ outside the walls of the church and into neglected areas. Crystal Enete wrote about her husband:

> *It was always difficult enough for him to get there with "Sammy" swinging onto the streetcars or squeezing in overcrowded busses... No suitcases are allowed on the suburban trains so he carried "Sammy" in a pillowcase. You can imagine how the astonished people stared at the suspicious looking bundle carried by the 'crazy American.' One hot Sunday he climbed one of those steep hills teeming*

with poor people living in shacks. The pastor said, 'Thirty thousand people live on this hill and these churches have been here for years. You are the first missionary to preach here.' It has warmed our hearts to hear the words of appreciation from our Brazilian brethren. Numbers have said, 'I was converted in one of your Vacation Bible Schools' or 'I responded to the call to preach in one of your meetings.' The seed has been sown.

In 1939, Enete published a book about his experiences called *Sammy Writes a Book*. This delightful collection of stories provides interesting snapshots from Enete's first fifteen years as a missionary. He ministered not only in Brazil, but also in Argentina, Chile, and Uruguay. Enete had another side to his creative ministry, which was raising missions' awareness and support in the USA. He kept church and camp audiences spell-bound with ventriloquism and multi-media presentations. He showed photographs and even made a motion picture about his work in South America called *Under Four Flags*.

Enete recognized the vast "missionary" potential of motion pictures long before the Board in Richmond. He passionately wrote about the future of films for missionary support predicting:

But it will come some day and will boost the information on missions like nothing else we have ever had. And when our people can see with their very own eyes the need, and hear with their very own ears the appeal, nothing can stop them from doing *what they can to alleviate the distress and darkness. Don't think for one moment that I am not giving full value to the work already done, but we could multiply it many fold. Then we will be helping the brethren to follow Christ's command when he said, "Lift up you eyes and <u>LOOK</u> on the field." Let's give them something to look at that will <u>demand</u> their attention.*

The Enetes faced numerous difficulties as they sought to carry out their ministry. William's unique methods frequently brought criticism from fellow missionaries, and his numerous journeys entailed expenses that were higher than those of a stationary missionary. The Enetes also had a trying misunderstanding during their furlough in 1939. Crystal memorably summed up the experience, *"The lamentable thing about missionaries is the fact that they are human: Get hot in the summer and cold in the winter, say Ouch when a pin pricks them."*

Their son Happy had been struggling with dysentery for three years until William decided that Happy needed medical treatment in the USA. This was the beginning of a great trial for the entire family. What they had hoped would be a short hospital stay for Happy became a six-year furlough (1941-1947) for the entire family. Finally, William, Crystal, and Joy were able to return to Brazil in December of 1947. Happy had improved enough to attend college at Baylor but was far from being well. He did marry a girl he met at Ridgecrest and fathered two sons, but he died of colon cancer at the age of twenty-eight. Happy's illness and death were a heavy burden for the entire family, but they rejoiced that his earthly sufferings were over. William informed the Board, *"Happy went to his heavenly home Saturday about high noon."*

William and Crystal broadened their evangelistic outreach during their final decade as Southern Baptist missionaries. William reported, *"The general evangelistic work is reaching many through meetings in the churches, auditoriums, in the open air and in day schools and colleges. It has been a glorious experience that they have heard the gospel so gladly, that the crowds have been larger than the auditoriums. In these crowds there have been many who have heard the gospel for the first time. Many hear, believe and accept all on one occasion, and the power of the gospel does the work."*

During this period the Enetes bought and outfitted a bus, which they named *LUCY*, to be used for evangelistic outreach. *LUCY* was a mobile platform for Uncle Billy and Sammy. It had speakers and lights to attract attention when they entered a town. It was also a mobile home for the Enetes. For several years, *LUCY* was an incredible missionary tool, and thousands of people heard the Gospel in areas that had been unreached. Apparently, *LUCY* was the object of criticism, and the Enetes were forced to sell it. Crystal summarized:

> *We have given our best in direct evangelism and have had the joy of seeing many turn to Jesus and the superabundant joy of hearing from pastors that they are baptizing many of these people. I am deeply grateful for the privilege of going with my husband on a three-month journey in our evangelistic bus before it was sold. The bus made it possible for us to go to distant places and yet enjoy nourishing*

food, pure water and nightly rest. We have been lifted above the painful effects of rumors, unofficial reports, and persecution, which will continue as long as missionaries are human.... Songs in the night have been sent, and we have had to look up as never before to One who never forsakes but sustains and gives grace to bear.

In their final years of full-time service, Crystal, who was an artist, began "one of her most rewarding activities—the painting of murals in the baptistries of Brazilian Baptist churches. Though people observing the process often feel some misgivings, as she directs her husband, "Uncle Billy" in the use of a spray gun, to paint clouds, sky or background, she invariably comes up with a baptistry scene which is both beautiful and so realistic that it seems that one should be able to wade out into the river she has so ably depicted."

William and Crystal Enete retired in 1958, after almost twenty-five years of missionary service. Their retirement was not the end of their ministry in Brazil as they returned many times for extended stays to share the Gospel. William suffered a heart attack in 1967, and after many months of declining health, he died. William had been God's instrument to lead many to faith in Jesus Christ. Near the end of his missionary career, William wrote, *"My heart wants to be young again, so I could give another life to Brazil. But this one is not finished yet and I think it would be wise to win many more souls for the Master."* William Enete was a pioneer who endured much criticism through the years, but he remained faithful to the end. Many in heaven will thank God for sending Uncle Billy and Sammy their way.

Uncle Billy and Sammy

Sammy writes a book

Uncle Billy and Sammy

Lula Whilden, missionary to South China

Chapter Eighteen

LULA WHILDEN

1846-1916
Evangelist to Destitute Women

"In the morning sow your seed, and at evening with-
hold not your hand, for you do not know which will
prosper, this or that, or whether both alike will be
good."   **Ecclesiastes 11:6**

Lula F. Whilden was born in Camden, South Carolina, in 1846.
Her father, Bayfield Whilden, was a Baptist pastor, and her
mother, Eliza Jane Whilden, was also a strong Christian with a
vibrant prayer life. Eliza Jane had a fervent missionary spirit, and
her prayers were saturated with petitions to God that her husband
would desire to serve as a missionary in China. She also constantly
prayed that her children would have the same missionary desire.
Bayfield was content being a pastor in the USA; however, six years
after their marriage, he applied to the Foreign Mission Board to
become a missionary. Eliza's prayers were being answered.

Bayfield W. Whilden had grown up in the historic First Baptist
Church of Charleston, South Carolina, and in preparation for going
overseas, the Whildens returned to Bayfield's home church. The

ladies of First Baptist sewed enough clothes for the three Whilden children (Jumelle, Lula, De Leon) to fill a gigantic travel trunk. The commissioning service for the Whilden family took place on October 16, 1848. The sermon text was Psalm 2:8, *"Ask of me, and I shall give thee the heathen for thine inheritance, and the utter-most parts of the earth for thy possession."* The gathering was "of deep and solemn interest," and it strengthened the hold that foreign missions "had taken upon the hearts and sympathies" of the people of First Baptist Church.

The family sailed from New York on the *Valpariso* on October 9, 1848. They arrived at their mission station in Canton, China, on February 23, 1849—a journey of over four months! Bayfield wrote, *"It is a source of unspeakable joy that I am permitted to labor any-where in the Lord's vineyard."* He wasted no time in getting to work. As soon as he had some small phrase in Chinese, he used it, *"Study the Bible, worship the true God, and believe in Jesus Christ."*

In a letter dated August 20, 1849, he wrote, *"Christ's command is obeyed, if the gospel is preached, even if no heart is affected. The work of the Church is to send missionaries; the work of the missionary is to sow the seed; the work of the Spirit is to cause the seed to spring up and bear fruit."* Certainly, a long and useful missionary career lay before such a consecrated servant, but God's ways are not our ways. His wife Eliza fell ill and died on February 20, 1850 (nine days shy of one year in Canton). Her final prayers were for her children *"to spend and be spent for the heathen."* She was laid to rest on French Island in the Pearl River beside Southern Baptists' first missionary, Samuel Clopton, who had passed away three years earlier.

Several months later, Bayfield returned to America with his three motherless children. He remarried and brought his second wife to Canton in 1853. Within two years, she began to lose her sight, and the couple was forced back to the States. Bayfield did not realize his dream of spending his life as a missionary, but as a pastor in the USA, he led numerous churches to have a missionary spirit.

Lula had experienced great sadness and upheavals in her young life; however, God was using those afflictions to shape in her a heart of immense compassion. Her mother had died, her stepmother had become blind, and her family had been tossed to and fro. What would become of Lula? At the age of seventeen, Lula was converted to Christ and baptized in Aiken, South Carolina. She completed her education at Greenville Female College (now merged with Furman University) in 1870. Upon graduation, she taught at the college for two years. She enjoyed it greatly, and that experience forged a close bond between her and that institution for the rest of her days.

Yet, Lula's heart was being drawn toward China. In fact, even while a student, her support of missions was strong. She wrote to Secretary James Taylor in Richmond in 1869, *"It is with unfeigned pleasure that I now enclose this humble offering ($5) for the benefit of Foreign Missions. I wish that it were in my power to contribute more. May even this under the blessing of God accomplish much good!"*

Lula wanted to give more than money. She wanted to give herself, but the Board's policy prohibited single women from being appointed. In each letter accompanying her monetary gifts, Lula gently pressed her case, *"Even if to me is denied the privilege of bearing the message of life to those who sit in 'darkness and in the shadow of death,' yet in my humble way I would strive to aid those whom God has thus highly favored."*

The Board had sent out one single female missionary, Harriet Baker, to Shanghai in 1850. The experiment did not go smoothly, and the Board decided to prohibit further single women missionaries. This policy remained firmly in place for almost twenty years. On July 1, 1871, the Board reversed its position and appointed Lula Whilden as a missionary to China. All missionaries must undergo a physical examination prior to being sent overseas. A medical doctor in South Carolina wrote, "This is to certify that I have examined Miss Louisa F. Whilden and find her to be 25 years old, about 4 feet 8 inches in height, average weight about 98 pounds." No one could have foreseen the enormous amount of good this tiny lady was getting ready to do!

Lula wrote the Board upon her appointment in 1871, *"There is something to me very sweet in the thought of being entirely dependent upon Jesus for my happiness for the remaining years of my life, and I know that having left all for him, he will be to me everything that I could desire. I trust that with God's spirit to fit me for the work, and His grace to sustain me in the performance of it, I may be able to labor for the eternal welfare of the heathen and that the Board may never regret its decision to send me. God's strength will be made perfect in my weakness."*

Lula's adult journey to China was vastly different from her childhood trip. In 1848, the journey had taken four months. In 1872, it took just over one month, and today, the same distance can be covered in less than twenty-four hours. She traveled with a party of eight missionaries, including her sister and brother-in-law, from

Baltimore to San Francisco by train and from California to Asia by steamer ship. They arrived in Canton on June 5, 1872. It must have been quite stirring to the young women to visit their mother's grave that bore the inscription: *"To Live is Christ, and to Die is Gain."* These young missionaries were *living answers* to their mother's *dying prayer*. Lula's sister Jumelle fell ill after only a few years in Canton, and she and her husband returned to America.

Lula began working with Mrs. Jane Graves in the establishment of the first Baptist school for girls in South China. Lula wrote, *"In these schools we gather together many heathen children who have been taught from infancy to bow the knee in idol worship—who have never seen a Bible, and have never heard of Jesus and His great salvation. Here they learn of Jesus as the only true God and the sinner's Saviour, are taught to pray to Him; and to sing hymns of praise to His name. The Bible is made one of their text books and its sacred teachings are treasured up in their memories while we pray that the Holy Spirit may apply them to their hearts."* Lula had a wonderful spiritual influence on the girls, and over the years, many of them turned from idols to serve the true and living God.

There was an old lady, who lived in a 3'x5' hut near the mission station. She survived by begging on the streets. Lula had offered her assistance and a kind word on many occasions. One day when the message reached Lula that the old lady was dying, she hurried to the little hut to tell her the story of Jesus and His dying on the cross for sinners. This happened early in Lula's missionary service, and she was concerned because she only had a beginner's knowledge of Chinese. Yet, as she spoke, the old woman's face beamed with understanding and joy, and she trusted Christ to save her. This was the first person in China that Lula led to Christ, but she was not the last. Lula was a gifted evangelist, who shared the Gospel with thousands and thousands over the next forty years.

God had uniquely graced Lula with a Christ-like compassion for the destitute. It was said of Lula, "The more neglected, the greater was her love." Lula was moved by the forlorn conditions of the thousands of women who lived on boats in the Pearl River. These "houseboats" were not much bigger than a rowboat. The people who lived on them were extremely poor and despised. Lula would pass from boat to boat, telling the women of Jesus Christ. They were shocked that anyone cared about them. It was clear to everyone who met Lula that she shared Christ, not merely because it was her duty, but out of a deep love for people. Her love was a powerful force, and many women responded by pouring out their hearts to this ambassador for Christ. As Lula talked with these world-weary women about heaven, *"there came a longing for the home where no tears are shed, the sorrowless home above. And they smiled because they hoped, through trust in Jesus, some day to find a welcome there."*

Lula was a boat-to-boat and house-to-house evangelist. Most of the sentences in her diary began with one of two words: *visited* or *went*. Hardly a day passed without Lula going somewhere to speak to someone about Jesus. She would often go to a place, start reading the Bible out loud, and then answer the questions the women asked. A diary entry from Christmas Day, 1879, reads, *"Visited first in the neighborhood. The woman with inflamed eyes was one of my most attentive listeners. She said, 'It is true, what you said yesterday. We worship block wooden images. I want to worship the Living God who made Heaven and earth.' She asked me if she prayed to Jesus, if He would help her to control her temper as she was irritable*

*and passionate. Another woman said, 'The words enter my heart.'
I was reading of some of Christ's teachings. Read at another place
across the river. It has been a busy but happy Christmas day. May
souls be granted me as my Saviour's gift."*

Another aspect of Lula Whilden's ministry was writing letters
back to America to foster the missionary spirit among Southern
Baptist women. Lula prodded, *"Does not your soul sometimes
thrill with joy as you look forward to a blissful eternity spent in
the home and presence of Jesus? Will you be content to go there
alone?"* Prayer was as important to Lula as breathing, and it was
an ever-open door of constant communication between her and
her Savior. She urged Chinese women to pray to Jesus for salvation, and she urged the Christian women in America to pray for
the salvation of those Chinese women. Lula implored, *"Oh, will
you not plead for these poor idolators who are daily passing into
eternity without a ray of hope beyond the tomb?"* She continued,
*"Disciple of Jesus you have power with God. In the name of your
crucified redeemer approach the Mercy Seat. Grasp the promises of
God with a strong faith and hold them up before His throne. Plead,
wrestle, agonize—refuse to let Him go until they are fulfilled."*

After ten years of service in China, Lula was worn down. She
returned to America in 1882 and hastened to the Southern Baptist
Convention, which was meeting in Greenville, South Carolina,
that year. After the convention, she was inundated with requests to
speak about her mission work in China. Because she felt *"through
these talks a deeper interest in China would be awakened, and
more constant, fervent prayer would be offered for its perishing
millions,"* she accepted seventy-one speaking engagements during
the course of that year. She said, *"The year of home work, added*

to ten years of overwork in China brought on such complete nervous prostration that the doctor said my return to China depended upon my giving up all missionary meetings and taking entire rest."

Lula had planned to be in America for a year and a half, but her physical breakdown caused that period to stretch into eight years. She lamented, *"These years of resting have been the most trying portion of my life. It is easier far to go forth to the rescue of the perishing, than to know that 'a million a month in China are dying without God,' and yet, through physical weakness, be compelled to sit still."* Some of those years were spent in rest, but Lula was not one to stop ministering.

She accepted an assignment with the Home Mission Board (today NAMB) to be its missionary to the several hundred Chinese living in Baltimore. She would walk from laundry to laundry sharing the Good News. Several older Chinese men became believers in the autumn of their lives. Lula wrote, *"I am trying faithfully to lead these souls to Jesus, but who can blame me that ever and anon there comes into my heart a deep and irrepressible longing to be once more among the heathen women and children of China, to leave the home work for home workers and go far hence to the heathen, where the souls of the unsaved are many and the messengers of salvation so sadly few."*

Finally, in 1890, Lula Whilden returned to Canton. Over the next quarter of a century, she continued her evangelistic outreach to the destitute. There was one group of females even lower than the boat women: blind singing girls. These girls were treated like slaves; they were often sold or given away by their families. They were piled into cramped dorms, where they were taught to sing. The singing was a ploy to get the attention of passing men. Lula explained, *"Their faces are painted and powdered. Handsomely dressed, with guitar in hand, they are taken into the streets at night. In the morning they return to the owner's house and the master receives the money secured at such a terrible cost."* Lula grieved, *"Not even the miserable beggar with his uncombed hair, filthy tattered garments, hollow eyes, and emaciated frame, is deserving of so much pity, though at first glance he awakens more. They are the miserable outcasts from society, and yet they have become so from no fault or through no wish of their own."*

Lula asked a blind eight-year-old girl what her name was. The girl responded, "Little Dog." Despite her blindness, her life had begun with parents who loved her. They both died, and she went to live with a grandfather, who saw her as a burden and sold her. Her owners were preparing her for a life of shame. Lula recounted, *"She was left alone in the house at night. Between midnight and morning her owners returned. For falling asleep and failing to answer to the first knock the child was tied up and whipped like a dog. They burned her body with lighted sticks; and at times compelled her to eat rice into which they had mixed pepper and tobacco."* Lula, who was moved to take the girl home with her, purchased Little Dog for ten dollars.

The girl was given a new name, Yan Teen, which means Grace and Mercy. Lula took many blind girls into her home and began to advocate for the building of a group home for blind girls. Through her efforts and the generosity of private donors, a home was built that could accommodate sixty girls. In addition, Lula started a school for them. The Mo Kwang School for the Blind was the first of its kind in all of China.

In 1909, Lula was in her early sixties and had been under appointment as a Southern Baptist missionary for thirty-seven years. She had become a living inspiration to her Southern Baptist sisters and brothers. The Convention marveled, "Miss Whilden does a work that is unique, and only eternity can reveal its results. She, in the cold, in the rain and in the burning sunshine, walks many miles, carrying 'the old, old story which is too sadly new to many,' into the homes of the heathen women... She has made this year over six hundred visits to heathen homes."

In 1914, as Lula was making evangelistic visits, she was attacked by thieves. She was severely beaten and robbed. This had happened to her before, but she was now seventy years of age, and the shock to her system was too much. She traveled to America to recover, entering the Baptist Hospital in Columbia, South Carolina. She continued to decline and for the final two months, she hardly spoke a coherent sentence until she had a visit from a missionary couple. They sang to her in Chinese "Jesus, Lover of my Soul." Lula stirred and responded in Chinese. Two weeks later, on September 26, 1916, Lula's spirit left her mortal body and entered the presence of her Savior. The hymn the missionaries sang to her was expressive of her heart and life. One verse says:

> *Thou, O Christ, art all I want*
> *More than all in Thee I find*
> *Raise the fallen, cheer the faint*
> *Heal the sick and lead the blind*

> *Just and holy is Thy name*
> *I am all unrighteousness*
> *False and full of sin I am*
> *Thou art full of truth and grace*

Jesus doesn't have favorites, but Miss Lula F. Whilden is probably an exception. South Carolina missions advocate, Janie Chapman, wrote that Lula Whilden was "the embodiment of the love of Christ for human souls." Lula left behind almost no worldly possessions, but after her death, an unpublished manuscript was found in her trunk. The pages were filled with the beautiful, simple stories of her sharing Christ with the destitute women of China. The Baptist women of South Carolina published her manuscript as *Life Sketches from a Heathen Land*. It manifests her one desire in life—to bring souls to Christ. May God grant us in coming days an army of Lula Whildens. Listen once again to Lula's heart, *"Life, at the longest, seems too short to devote to such a work. O that the Lord would send forth more laborers into the harvest."*

Young Lula Whilden

ACKNOWLEDGMENTS

My dear friend, Shelia Thompson, painted the beautiful artwork on the cover of this book. Shelia is a wonderful artist, as well as a devoted Christian. She has been greatly supportive of this project from the beginning. Shelia, thank you! I love your painting. It is perfect.

The Archives of the International Mission Board (SBC) have made it possible for me to access the historical sources used in this book. Everyone in that department—Scott, Jim, Beverly, Becky, and Kyndal—has been very welcoming and incredibly helpful throughout this process. They do a vitally important work in preserving the record of our past missionary efforts. As Southern Baptists, we owe them a great debt of gratitude. Thank you, Archives!

My brother, John Brady, has been my ongoing dialogue partner during the writing of these missionary stories. John, I treasure our conversations, and I delight that we share the same passion for seeing the Gospel of Jesus Christ reach the nations. Thank you for your encouragement and enthusiasm for this project.

My wife, Jennifer Jennings Brady, has been a rock of support, in countless ways, throughout this long journey. Jennifer, I could not have done any of this, nor would I have wanted to, without you. You are the sweetness in my life. I love you!

Thank you to everyone who prayed for me during this project. Your interest, support, and helpful suggestions have blessed me greatly.

Above all, I would like to acknowledge my Lord and Savior, Jesus Christ. I long for Him to be known and loved by the peoples of this earth. If this book contributes to making Christ known, I will be pleased. May the nations acknowledge *"the bread of God is he who comes down from heaven and gives life to the world."*

PHOTOGRAPH CREDITS

There were several institutions that provided me with photographs for this book. However, the overwhelming majority of them come from the collection of the International Mission Board (SBC).

xii John and Carrie Lake (Photo courtesy of the International Mission Board). Hereafter, the International Mission Board referred to as IMB

12 Tai-Kam Leper Colony under construction (Photo courtesy of the IMB)

13 Tai-Kam Island from boat (Photo courtesy of the IMB)

14 Tai-Kam residents (Photo courtesy of the IMB)

15 Tai-Kam men waving (Photo courtesy of the IMB)

16 John Lake (Photo courtesy of the IMB)

17 John Lake (Photo courtesy of the IMB)

31 Samuel Clopton Jr. (1847-1905), son of the first Southern Baptist missionary (Photo courtesy of the Virginia Baptist Historical Society)

48 Bradys leave for Guyana in 1962 (Personal collection of the author: DJB)

61 Otis W. Brady Jr. (Personal collection of the author: DJB)

62 Guyana in the 1960s (Personal collection of the author: DJB)

62 Stabroek Market in Georgetown, Guyana, in the 1960s (Personal collection of the author: DJB)

63 Otis, Martha, David, and Jennifer in Belize in the 1980s (Personal collection of the author: DJB)

64 John Day Jr., missionary to Liberia (Public Domain)

74 Thomas and Laurenna Bowen, missionaries to Nigeria (Photo courtesy of the IMB)

90 T.A. and Mary Reid, missionaries to Nigeria (Photo courtesy of the IMB)

96 Matthew Yates, missionary to Shanghai (Photo courtesy of the IMB)

106 Matthew, Eliza, and Annie Yates (Photo courtesy of the IMB)

107 Yates, towering pioneer (Screenshot from the public domain book: *Yates the Missionary* by Charles E. Taylor)

108 Landrum Holmes, missionary to Shandong Province, China (Screenshot from the public domain book: *Shantung: The Sacred Province of China*, compiled and edited by Robert Forsyth Coventry, 1912)

118 Landrum and Sallie Holmes wedding photo (Photo courtesy of Deborah Guiher Chamblee provided by the IMB)

132 Solomon Ginsberg, missionary to Brazil (Photo courtesy of the IMB)

138 Solomon Ginsberg for Brazil (Photo courtesy of the IMB)

139 Solomon Ginsberg at his desk (Public Domain)

139 Printing shop of the Mildmay Mission to the Jews in London (Screenshot from a yearly report of the Mildmay Mission to the Jews)

140 Solomon Ginsberg (Photo courtesy of the IMB)

142 Erik Alfred Nelson, missionary to the Amazon (Photo courtesy of the IMB)

152 Riverboat in the Amazon (Photo courtesy of the IMB)

153 Erik and Ida Nelson (Photo courtesy of the IMB)

154 Erik Nelson (Photo courtesy of the IMB)

155 Erik Nelson (Photo courtesy of the IMB)

156 Erik Nelson in his motorboat (Photo courtesy of the IMB)

156 The Buffalo in a far-flung lake of the Amazon (Photo courtesy of the IMB)

157 Eric Nelson preparing for a 1,500 journey up the Amazon (Photo courtesy of the IMB)

158 George Holcombe Lacy, missionary to Mexico (Photo courtesy of the IMB)

166 The Lacy family (Photo from Chastain's *Thirty Years in Mexico*)

167 George Lacy (Photo courtesy of the IMB)

168 T.W. Ayers, medical missionary to North China (Photo courtesy of the IMB)

180 T.W. Ayers (Photo courtesy of the IMB)

181 Dr. Ayers with medals awarded to him by the Chinese government (Photo courtesy of the IMB)

181 Dr. Ayers with Chinese medical school graduates (Ayers Family Papers, MS248, Special Collections & Archives, Z. Smith Reynolds Library, Wake Forest University, Winston-Salem, NC, USA)

182 Dr. Ayers with a young patient (Photo courtesy of the IMB)

183 Monument in North China honoring Dr. Ayers (Ayers Family Papers, MS248, Special Collections & Archives, Z. Smith Reynolds Library, Wake Forest University, Winston-Salem, NC, USA)

184 William W. Enete Sr., missionary to Brazil (Photo courtesy of the IMB)

193 Uncle Billy and Sammy (Photo courtesy of the IMB)

194 Sammy writes a book (Photograph by author—DJB—of the front cover of *Sammy Writes a Book* by Me)

195 Uncle Billy and Sammy (Photo courtesy of the IMB)

196 Lula Whilden, missionary to South China (Photo courtesy of the IMB)

208 Young Lula Whilden (Photo courtesy of the IMB)

CPSIA information can be obtained
at www.ICGtesting.com
Printed in the USA
BVHW030017240623
666304BV00002B/232